Charles C. Anderson   L. D. Travis

PSYCHOLOGY
AND THE
LIBERAL CONSENSUS

This volume presents a carefully reasoned, rigorous critique of mainline academic psychology. From the professional beginnings of their discipline, contend the authors, American psychologists have made two promises: that psychology would be treated as a natural science and that its application to social—mainly educational—reform would be as effective as that of the more physical sciences to technological change. Underlying these promises is the "liberal consensus," the belief that social problems are to be solved by improvements in educational methods. Put to the test during the affluence of the 1950s and 1960s— the years of the liberal consensus—these promises were never kept, maintain the authors. Their provocative study provides a variety of reasons why the goal was unattained, and is even unattainable.

The book will be of interest to psychologists, sociologists, professional educators, and students of social change.

Charles C. Anderson, Professor of Educational Psychology, University of Alberta, is the author of many professional papers and co-author of Readings in Cognitive Psychology. *He holds the Ph.D. degree from Cambridge University.*

LeRoy D. Travis, Department of Educational Psychology, University of British Columbia, has published professional papers on memory development, personality, and educational psychology. He holds the Ph.D. degree.

PSYCHOLOGY
AND THE
LIBERAL CONSENSUS

Charles C. Anderson   L. D. Travis

PSYCHOLOGY
AND THE
LIBERAL CONSENSUS

Wilfrid Laurier University Press

Canadian Cataloguing in Publication Data

Anderson, Charles C. (Charles Campbell), 1923-
 Psychology and the liberal consensus

Bibliography: p.
Includes index.
ISBN 0-88920-127-7

1. Psychology. 2. Psychology – Methodology. I. Travis,
LeRoy Douglas. II. Title.

BF38.5.A52   150.1'8   C83-098530-1

Cover design: Polygon Design Limited

Copyright © 1983

WILFRID LAURIER UNIVERSITY PRESS
Waterloo, Ontario, Canada N2L 3C5

83 84 85 86 4 3 2 1

CONTENTS

ACKNOWLEDGEMENTS

I am grateful to my sister, Mrs. L. Anderson of Balnagowan, Ozshott, Surrey, England, for her generous help and encouragement during the preparation of this manuscript, and to Beth Cunningham, a graduate student at the University of Alberta, for her help with the indices. Thanks are also due to John Harker, Editor of the *Canadian Journal of Edmonton,* for his permission to incorporate in the book some material from "The Bogus Science," published in that periodical.

This book has been published with the help of a grant from the Social Science Federation of Canada, using funds provided by the Social Sciences and Humanities Research Council of Canada.

Charles C. Anderson

I want to thank my wife, Anne Travis, for her able assistance with the indices and for her patience. Thanks are also extended to Claudio Violato for his help and to C.C.A. for his example and generosity.

LeRoy D. Travis

1 / INTRODUCTION: THE THESIS

The theme of this discourse is the sudden rise and development of psychology as a science designed to solve social problems by its application to education. This plan of bringing about social reform by conceptual change was unique in America, the "redeemer society" in which members of political parties and other ruling agencies were concerned more with material advantages and spoils than with the principled and direct attack on the social problems arising from their pursuit—racial discrimination, slum-ridden cities, the use by "captains of industry" of paramilitary forces to exploit labour and of money to corrupt political representatives at all levels, and the absence of concern for the common needs of ordinary people.

The solution to this conflict between the redeemer society and the ravages of its economic system had always taken the form of championing conceptual change, initially of a theological sort, instead of social change. However, with the successful scientific and technological advances in the late nineteenth and early twentieth centuries, the conceptual change was increasingly based on the hope that the new psychological science and its educational nostrums would somehow help the existing social order to get rid of the social crises that increasingly plagued it.

It will be shown that this is a vain hope because psychology in the form of theory or fragmented concepts is not a science in any sense of that term (Anderson, 1981), and because its advice to educators, necessarily bearing on changes in the curriculum rather than on improvements in staff, the school environment and its social milieu, is futile. Different approaches to psychology will be presented as illustrations of these points.

A. The Redeemer Society and Social Change

At the time of writing when the candidates for election to the office of President of the United States are a peanut farmer and a former actor in second-rate movies, American social intellectuals are more than ever con-

1

cerned about the process which brought about such a dismal state of affairs. Sanford (1980) points out that the presidential nominating procedure is not working well, never has done so in the last century, but it is, at least in theory, one of America's great contributions to politics. "Presidential nominating procedures should exude confidence in people and their capacity for self-government. That is America's indispensable message to the world, and our immutable obligation to our heritage" (Sanford, 1980, p. 29). Leaving aside the inconsistencies in this statement and Sanford's three suggestions for change in the nominating process, we should like to concentrate on that "heritage," Tuveson's (1968) "redeemer society," described as follows:

> Chosen race, chosen nation; millennial-utopian destiny for mankind, a continuing war between good (progress) and evil (reaction) in which the United States is to play a starring role as world redeemer—surely such an idea must be religious in origin (Tuveson, 1968, pp. vii-viii).

According to certain founding Protestant sects, the young Republic was to inaugurate a new heaven on earth. Providence had designed the American settlements to emancipate "the slavish part of mankind all over the earth" (p. 25), the slavery being the product of living under monarchs and priests (p. 24). Progress towards the new society was of a very secular sort—the end of wars, the improvement in health (p. 62) and the adequate provision of material needs for everybody (p.61)—supported by scientific discovery and technological innovation (pp. 67-68) which made material advancement inevitable. Of course there were problems, increasingly obvious as the nineteenth century advanced: corruption of every sort (p. 163); the plight of the American blacks (pp. 162-163); the great wave of immigrants, discriminated against unjustifiably (Baran and Sweezy, 1966, pp. 248-249); and the open conflict, manifested only obliquely on the political scene, between the rich and the poor (Lawson, 1971, pp. 19-20).

The only tolerable solution to these problems was to work within the parameters of the given social order and to develop private solutions to social problems. American educators like Horace Mann and Henry Barnard supported universal, compulsory education because they believed it would promote social mobility, end poverty and "become an agent of social reformation" (Lasch, 1975, p. 50). This kind of long-term incremental educational change was supported by the beneficiaries of the social system whose interests it would never damage (Hodgson, 1976, p. 25). For example, Dewey's progressive educational ideas tried out in the Laboratory School in Chicago (1896-1914), the Gary Plan in Indiana (1908-15) and the Dalton Plan in Massachusetts (1919), were sufficiently meretricious to be preferred to the more dangerous political and economic movements at the turn of the century (Lawson, 1971, pp. 85-86; Karier, 1966a, pp. 92-93).

The social predicament was considerable: how could the vast number of immigrants, poor and speaking a foreign tongue, be socialized into accepting the ideals of an American democracy besieged by the crises of political corruption, race relations and deteriorating cities (Hofstadter, 1963, p. 2; Mills, 1959, p. 308)? Much worse was the fact that school systems have never had the power or the prestige to carry out this sizeable task. They were characterized by "underpaid teachers, overcrowded classrooms, double-schedule schools, broken-down school buildings, inadequate facilities..." (Hofstadter, 1966, p. 300) and poorly-trained (or untrained) teachers who dealt with slow learners only by nonpromotion and punishment (Goodenough, 1950, p. 18) with the result that, according to a 1908 study by Thorndike, large numbers of students were lodged in the lower grades (p. 16). The many curriculum problems provoked only disagreement. The source of these problems (and of their social counterparts) was the historical unwillingness of Americans to be taxed for social purposes. In a fine passage, Galbraith (1958) notes that "A community decision to have a new school means that the individual surrenders the necessary amount, willy-nilly, in his taxes. But if he is left with that income, he is a free man. He can decide between a better car or a television set" (Galbraith, 1958, pp. 209-210).

However, early in the twentieth century, a concept emerged which seemed to obviate the need for increased taxation to improve performance in schools by providing better buildings and a staff that was better paid and with superior qualifications. The spate of uninformed and contrary opinions about educational issues would be replaced by a transformation of these issues into psychological hypotheses to be falsified or supported by using scientific methods (Joncich, 1961, p. 53). The principles of teaching and learning were to be based on the new science of psychology which, so it was hoped, might be applied to human performance as successfully as the natural sciences and their technological counterparts. This was the position taken by Ladd (1894) in his presidential address to the first meeting of the American Psychological Association in 1892. "This association is formed in the interest of psychology as a science ... the science of psychology may be expected to make large contributions toward the improvement of the art and practice of teaching" (Ladd, 1894, p. 19). Ladd goes on to claim that the stable principles of psychology as science will help the person whose training in mere "pedagogics" cannot prevent the children from being unnecessarily backward in educational achievement.

> One of the most important helps to improvement must come through the instruction of the teachers of these children in the principles of a truly scientific psychology. And such instruction must emanate from the highest expert sources, and penetrate to the lowest strata and the remotest regions in the public school system. It can never come in the form of half-baked treatises put forth by writers who, however seemingly successful they have been in practice, have no scientific understanding of the principles on which their own—too often merely apparent—success has been based (p. 20).

And Thorndike regarded psychology as part of a science which was "the only sure foundation for social progress" (Joncich, 1968, p. 4).

In retrospect, it is difficult to believe that eminent psychologists (Baldwin, Cattell, Judd, Ladd, Thorndike and Watson) thought they could provide authoritative answers to social and educational problems (Boring, 1929, p. 551) because the precise laws of the natural sciences derived from a study of the physical universe, could not readily be applied to the under-standing of active human beings with their capacity for changing the environment and for making value judgments. It is a fair guess that psychologists were fatally attracted to the important rank of social and educational reformers partly because of the honorific status of being scientists and partly because the alternative political and economic approaches to social change were unacceptable. Indeed, Alexander (1976) has noted these approaches provoked authorities into repressive and unconstitutional measures. For example, Weinstein (1967) comments on the remarks made in 1908 by a notorious socialist agitator. "Debs opposed capitalism because 'It's wrong. It's inherently unjust, inhuman, unintelligent, and it cannot last.' Graft, corruption, crime and cruelty were 'evidences of its weaknesses and failure; the signs that it is breaking down'" (Weinstein, 1967, p. 11). Clearly this would never do. Some kind of social change had to be achieved by an educational system reformed by psychological science. This had always been Dewey's position (1897, pp. 15-17; 1916, p. 24) and it was no accident that the first Rockefeller, widely detested in the first decades of the twentieth century (Collier and Horowitz, 1976, p. 5), gave a sizeable endowment to Teachers College in 1902 (Joncich, 1968, pp. 189-190).

Two types of solutions to these problems which became worse during the late nineteenth and early twentieth centuries were theoretically possible. First, there were those propounded by applied psychologists like Thorndike and those which might emerge from the development of a new psychological science systematically built in the laboratory by the experimental methods of the natural sciences. Second, teachers themselves, encouraged by some of Dewey's (1897; 1916) apparently radical ideas, might be called on to sponsor direct educational intervention designed to offset the unpleasant features of the Depression. The latter plan was unrealistic and, when used in the 1930s, was such an unmitigated failure that only the former has been contemplated regularly.

B. Science, Society, and Education

Cattell (1890), working in London with Galton, wrote an early piece on the value of using mental tests in which he managed to confuse causal or conditional laws, labelled Science 1, by Anderson (1981), with probabilistic laws (Science 2) based on any sort of correlational analysis:

> Psychology cannot attain the certainty and exactness of the physical sciences, unless it rests on a foundation of experiment and measurement. . . . Experimental psychology is likely to take a place in the educational plan of our schools and universities. . . . It teaches accurate observation and correct reasoning in the same way as the other natural sciences (Cattell, 1980, pp. 373-77).

For Cattell psychological science largely meant giving mental tests and working out their intercorrelations to establish probabilistic laws, a characteristic of all science according to Pearson (1890, p. 113), an associate of Galton. Later mental testers aided by such statistical laws, assessed the performance of students, selected them for an appropriate education and diagnosed learning difficulties. However, as will be noted, the business of using mental tests as an applied solution to educational problems was a dangerous trade even when it was not regarded as a support for the status quo (Karier, 1976b, p. 130).

Cattell's lack of discrimination between the two sciences was reflected in the work of Thorndike, his protege at Columbia. Thorndike considered his famous laws of learning as causal laws (Science 1), and himself a behavioural scientist who disliked "the mind" as an explanatory concept (Joncich, 1968, p. 273). A few years later he was converted to Cattell's ideas about mental testing (Thorndike, 1904), and he spent much of his life devising, administering and providing norms for tests of all kinds. His speculation that "intelligence" was a measure of the physiological bonds or connections in the brain now seems merely frivolous. It earned the wrath of Watson (1959, p. 109) but was routinely ignored by other behaviourists. Thorndike's confusion about causal and statistical laws is revealed in his treatment of determinism. In a 1909 paper dealing with Darwins's contribution to psychology, he remarked that "Our intellects and characters are no more subjects for magic, crude or refined, than the ebb and flow of the tides. Thus, at last, man may become ruler of himself as well as the rest of nature" (in Joncich, 1961, p. 45). And by 1940 he was supporting "the freedom of a person from domination by circumstances" (1940, p. 175) with the argument that "If, by chance, I . . . knew that my thoughts, feelings and actions were as inevitable as the pull of magnet on steel, I would thereby enormously increase my power to change my fate" (pp. 173-174). Thorndike did not appear to realise that the large errors of measurement revealed in mental testing research combined with a lack of a coherent theoretical structure which characterised even experimental psychology of a behavioristic sort, ruled out of court the assumption of determinism and of the causal laws of the natural sciences. To put it another way, using phraseology from quantum theory, the class of phenomena characterised by indeterminancies— and psychology certainly belongs to that category—yield only statistical laws (Platt, 1966, p. 17) which are consistent with the idea that people are not totally slaves to circumstances.

C. Probabilistic Science and Heredity

Thorndike acquired not merely Galton's interest in mental tests but also his belief in the hereditarian basis of intelligence and in "eugenics," the improvement of human stock by selective breeding (with its racial overtones). "No well-informed and sensible persons," he wrote in his last book (1940), "object to the general principle of eugenics. . ." (Thorndike, 1940, p. 194), especially the sterilization of mental defectives, of whom a disproportionately great number were "American Negroes" (p. 148). Thorndike believed that the practice of eugenics would indirectly create social progress to a much greater degree than "social education," a term he uses pejoratively. This line of research into mental testing and its probabilistic laws was always under attack in the United States where progress was defined as an equal opportunity of receiving an education which would equip a person for social and occupational improvement. This progress could not be seen if groups of people began their schooling with an inferior or superior genetic capacity which reduced or increased their opportunity to acquire an adequate education. Accordingly, the mental testing line of research and its professional use came under increasing attack with the passage of time.

D. Causal Laws and Determinism

Unlike Cattell and Thorndike, some psychologists saw that the cogency and power of a natural science lay in its laws which permit the control of the environment by predicting beforehand the conditions to be imposed to guarantee a desired result. Only behaviouristic psychologists (materialists) could have assumed that human behaviour was predictable and explainable in terms of these conditional or causal laws of Science 1. For example, Pavlov, heir to a long tradition of Russian anti-clerical materialism and full determinism (McLeish, 1975, p. 20. p. 70, p. 83), treated psychology as Science 1 by interpreting psychological functions in terms of physiological processes (Kaplan, 1966, pp. 345-346). Man was "a system—roughly speaking, a machine—like every other system subject to the inescapable and uniform laws of nature . . ." (p. 349). However, the range of Pavlov's theorizing is very restricted. Zener (1937) showed that a conditioned dog will, if unharnessed, cease to salivate on the presentation of the conditioned stimulus, and will move towards the pan in which its food is normally kept—and there is also the fact that Pavlov's theory of brain functioning was at odds with what was known of neurophysiology in his own day (Gray, 1979, pp. 102-103).

In America, Watson's behaviourism was of a programmatic, rough-and-ready sort, more of a call to action than a system. This is evident in his (very American) advice to a mother.

> I am trying to dangle in front of you a verbal stimulus which, if acted upon, will gradually change this universe. For the universe will change if you bring up your children in behavioristic freedom. . . . Will not these children in turn, with their better ways of living and thinking, replace us as society and in turn bring up their children in a still more scientific way, until the world finally becomes a place fit for human habitation? (Watson, 1928, pp. 303-304).

Although Watson wrote many of his later articles in popular magazines, his influence was negligible partly because his mature life was spent in advertising during the Depression and partly because his work was polemical rather than experimental. For Hull, he was a lost leader in the vanguard of the struggle for the development of psychology as a natural science.

Hull was the real Science 1 psychologist in America. In his *Idea Books* (1930), fragments of which were published in 1962, he recorded his belief that the success of natural science and technology had made feasible a systematic science:

This country is clearly on the upgrade. It is gathering momentum and power at a rapid rate. Even now it dominates the world in some things. The intangible exhilaration from this is likely to be of considerable advantage. Moreover, the temper of the rising generation is naturalistic in the extreme. The great modern wealth is founded on the application of science. The drift towards naturalism among scholars is decided. The great vogue of the crude Watsonian behaviorism shows how things are drifting. The time is evidently here for a searching naturalistic account of the manner that men acquire the various types of knowledge and the nature of this knowledge, done in the modern manner (Hull, 1962, p. 835).

The "modern manner" was Hull's preference for explaining behaviour in terms of stimuli and responses, large and small. "The strength of Hull's predilections for peripheralism seems generally reflected in his writing by a tendency to keep out of the brain everything he can get into the afferent or efferent segments of the nervous system" (Koch, 1954, p. 11). Moreover, he believed that a modern Science 1 psychology required laws expressed in "quasi-mathematical terms" (Hull, 1935, p. 498) and its author's approach should be as deterministic as that of any conventional scientist. By 1930 Hull noted that some human functions could be simulated by a machine (Hull, 1962, p. 820). One way of getting rid of subjectivism, he recommends in his *Principles of Behavior*, "is to regard, from time to time, the behaving organism as a completely self-maintaining robot. It is a wholesome and revealing exercise to consider the various general problems in behavior dynamics which must be solved in the design of a truly self-maintaining robot" (Hull, 1943, p. 17). The conceptual and empirical weaknesses of Hull's influential theories were exposed by Koch (1954) and it was left to Skinner to carry on the Science 1 tradition by using a new behaviour system which resembled his 1938 version only by the retention of the concept of an operational definition and by disregarding the physical as well as the conceptual nervous systems because they could not be measured or observed reliably. As he remarked in a crisp later comment, "The science I am discussing is the investigation of the relation between behavior and the enivronment ..." (Skinner, 1975, p. 48). Skinner produced the only Science 1 law known, a formula for predicting the rate at which a half-starved pigeon will peck a bar to obtain grain pellets (Ferster and Skinner, 1957).

An exception might be made in the case of the Law of Effect. Originally defined by Thorndike as a satisfying (or unsatisfying) state of affairs which metaphorically strengthened (or weakened) the previous S-R connection (Thorndike, 1913, p. 4), it was later used to refer to an astonishing variety of stimulus events (Thorndike, 1940, pp. 8-9). Skinner took the Law of Effect out of this conceptual bog by defining it operationally. Reinforcement became a stimulus which influenced the probability of recurrence of a preceding response above or below a certain basal rate (Skinner, 1953, pp. 72-73). Like the older Thorndike (1932, p. 46), Skinner emphasized positive reinforcement, which *increased* the probability of recurrence of the previous behaviour. This practice, however, entailed value judgments beyond the realm of behavioural science and technology: who or what agency was to administer the reinforcer to promote and sustain what kind of behaviour?

Skinner's elimination of the "homunculus" problem and his implicit claim to be a Science 1 psychologist was, paradoxically, one reason why he has been rejected by social intellectuals and their lay counterparts. Despite the fact that planning and control is exercised by authorities of some sort without the consent of the "autonomous" man (Galbraith, 1979), they disliked the idea that people were a hostage to their environment. This would have denied the American dream of progress, of material and personal improvement described by Heilbroner (1959):

> We are naturally sympathetic to ideas which stress the plasticity and promise, the openness of the future, and impatient with views which emphasize the 'fatal' aspect of human affairs. We strive to see in the challenges which beset not obstacles but opportunities. In a word, we are an optimistic people (Heilbroner, 1959, p. 16).

Over and above the logical and empirical flaws in behaviourism as Science 1 psychology (Mackenzie, 1978), its claim on the attention of educators has been slight. Youngsters in a classroom cannot be as readily manipulated as Pavlov's dogs, Thorndike's wild cats, Guthrie's tame cats and Skinner's rats, pigeons and chickens. Indeed, even with organisms at this relatively low phyletic level, it is often difficult to tell who is manipulating whom (Postman, 1979). Accordingly, it is not surprising that after Hull's death in 1952 the debilitating constraints of a deterministic behaviourism, fashionable during the 1930s and 1940s, was displaced by a new cognitive psychology more attractive than its dominant ancestor, Gestalt psychology which, despite the work of Tolman (1932) and some cogent neurological research (Lashey and Ball, 1929), had made little headway in America (Thorndike declared that he could not understand it). The newer variety with its heavier emphasis on verbal rather than spatial functions, promised solutions to the educational and social problems that emerged during the 1950s (Lewis, 1965, p. 23) and mustered the kind of experimental support that could not be derided too much by the Science 1 enthusiasts.

E. Educational Activists

Social intellectuals, in an indirect and dismissive way, tolerated Dewey's view that teachers were a force for social change. People who seriously believed with Dewey that social change was a product of a change in youngsters learning to be autonomous people, scientists and democrats who made collective discoveries, were regarded as harmless cranks (Lasch, 1975, p. 53). However, when it became clear that there was no forseeable solution to the unpleasant features of the Depression—high unemployment, low productivity and the emergence of dissident groups like Communists and Nazis—a more radical group of his followers began to urge teachers to play a direct part in developing a new society by teaching students about the evils of capitalism and the shape of a new social order that would replace it (Bowers, 1969, p. 18). Specifically, teachers were asked to decide between supporting the "business values" of the older society and the collective values and ownership of the means of production and exchange that were the advertised features of the new hypothetical reformed society (p. 18). True to his liberal outlook, Dewey himself wavered; he liked the radical position that teachers should not transmit received values and opinion, but he disliked the direct teaching of alternatives (he considered this "propaganda") and the loss of his concept of a child-centered school, guided by democracy and experimentation.

The New Frontier, beginning in 1932 as the journal of the radical group, published suggestions about the new society, particularly the proposed redistribution of wealth; but its editors and writers were unaware of the fact that teachers had neither the status nor the authority to begin the task of reconstruction. They had no influence on American Teacher, the official organ of the American Federation of Teachers; nor on the labour movement which did not want to be led by teachers; nor on Communists who regarded schools as mirroring bourgeois values (pp. 143-144); nor on the young economists with some access to the corridors of power in Washington who were trying to promote the idea of government spending as the only realistic solution to the economic and industrial problems of the day (Galbraith, 1972, pp. 48-49). The economists, far from advocating teaching about the class struggle and the inequities of an economic system which had broken down in a country naturally wealthy, were helping to bail out that system. Another factor ignored by the radicals was the gathering of reactionary forces headed by the House Committee on Un-American Activities which was established in 1938. While Dewey was worrying about indoctrination and the class struggle in the schools (Bowers, p. 154), the Committee was aggressively investigating not merely the influence and existence of Communists but also aspects of Roosevelt's New Deal which involved public spending and government intervention in industrial activity (Goodman, 1969, p. 32). The power of this Committee to terrorize school teachers was not apparent until 1959 (p. 425), but its hunting down of dissident teachers began as early as 1940 (pp. 89-90). The idea of social change in America which ran counter to "business values" was seen by realists to be a dead issue early in the 1940s when unemployment decreased and productivity expanded as a function of military spending, subscriptions to The New Frontier declined and, after the Hitler-Stalin pact of 1939, reformers fought to prevent Communists from infiltrating some local branches of the American Federation of Teachers. As Bowers points out, the radicals did not understand the conditions which made teachers useless as reformers: their lack of job security and the preponderance among them of women who preferred to teach the curriculum rather than any "social radicalism" (p. 165).

In the 1950s the educational activists were silenced completely by the march of certain events: it became increasingly difficult during the McCarthy years to describe a middle way between the apparently flourishing United States and the Communist powers. So blacks, and other Americans alarmed by Sputnik, settled for equal educational opportunity which, so they believed, would lead to social mobility and equality. The educational activists of the future would be students in the 1960s.

F. The Liberal Consensus

In the relatively affluent American society after the Second World War (Hacker, 1971, pp. 17-18) members of the "liberal consensus," which combined an anti-Communist foreign policy with a technocratic approach to social problems, believed that professional students of people might come in handy as social technologists. Hodgson (1976) describes the credo of consensus members.

> Social problems can be solved like industrial problems. The problem is first identified; programs are designed to solve it by government enlightened by social science; money and other resources—such as trained people—are then applied to the problem as inputs; the outputs are predicted: the problem will be solved (p. 76).

Clearly the early psychologists with their theoretical in-fighting and back-to-the-drawingboard attitude typified by Spence (1959, pp. 89-90), an ageing Hullian, could never accomplish this task, nor could the improvements in test theory and construction during the war years (Goodenough, 1950, pp. 459-502; Gulliksen, 1974, p. 252). What was wanted was a new curriculum, backed by a new sort of psychological science, which would provide equal educational opportunity to the threatening blacks and keep the Communist enemies at bay. Accordingly, a liberal supply of research grants—Koch (1974, p. 21) put the figure at $326 million (not including Head Start) for 1967 alone—became available to psychologists who could hitch their research to potential educational improvements such as a reduction in illiteracy, and an increase in IQ, the stimulation of "creativity" and a more effective approach to teaching mathematics, the physical and biological sciences and technology. No attempt was made, indeed could be made, to improve the hiring of superior and better-paid teachers, the elimination of slums and the rehabilitation of their inhabitants. As always, the social change envisaged was not institutional but conceptual, a "conceptual revolution" or "revolution in consciousness" (Hitchcock, 1969, p. 4).

2 / OVERTURES TO ORTHODOXY: COGNITIVE THEORY AND COMPUTER PROGRAMMES

A. The Two Problems

The function of the natural scientist—and cognitive psychologists have usually tried to sneak into this category—is to construct a scientific system from the axioms of which laws can be deduced to account for observed regularities (Harre, 1974, p. 241). The cogency and power of such a system lies in its laws, expressed in mathematical terms or rough and less precise equivalents. An example of such a law is F=mxa (force = mass x acceleration) and one problem for cognitive scientists is how to manipulate their important cognitive processes, postulated as a middle term between the stimulus and the response, to achieve the desired behaviour and to derive the much-prized "laws." According to Skinner, these "mental events," unobservable, private, and inferential, were pseudo-explanations which often could be concocted to suit the explicanda (the events to be explained) (Skinner, 1953, p. 27) of which the most extreme case is the attribution of a *virtus dormitiva* to opium to account for its power to put people to sleep (Dennett, 1978, p. 56). A special case of such circular reasoning or superfluous description is the surreptitious postulation of an "inner man" or "homunculus" whose function is to provide an explanation which will not be explained in turn (Skinner, 1972, p. 11). An example would be perception described in terms of an internal cognitive map or model; who provides us with this map and how does he have the power to do so? (Dennett, 1978, p. 122). Another example would be the pseudo-explanation of creative performance in terms of a special disposition of "creativity."

Skinner wants to shift control from the autonomous inner man to the environment, in terms of which explanations can be found like those in the natural sciences. "Science does not de-humanize man; it de-humunculizes—only by dispossessing him can we turn to the real causes of human behavior. Only then can we turn from the inferred to the natural, from the inaccessible to the manipulable" (p. 191).

This leads to the second problem, the social contexts in which any psychological science, particularly a cognitive one, can incorporate representations of that society which will help promote social reform. The difficulty of accomplishing such a task can be made clear by recalling that psychologists, especially those attempting to devise a basic theory, at best make only passing references, usually inaccurate, to aspects of their society, past or present. The likely dilemma, then, is that if cognitive psychology is moved as closely as possible to another discipline that could justifiably be labelled a science, the strategy would appear to solve the "homunculus" problem at the expense of dealing with the more intractable social considerations. This was the fate of the research into the computer simulation of performance.

B. Cognitive Psychology and Computing Science

The main source of the new cognitive psychology was the scientific and technological developments (the programming of the early digital computers and the associated development of communication theory) arising from the Second World War. Craik's (1943) original speculation is worth noting because of its clarity.

> My hypothesis then is that thought models, or parallels, reality—that its essential feature is not "the mind, " "the self, " sense data, nor propositions but symbols, and that this symbolism is largely of the same kind as that which is familiar to us in mechanical devices which aid thought and calculation (Craik, 1943, p. 57).

This simulation of thought in computer programmes was remarkably successful after von Neumann's 1948 discovery that codes, sets of instructions describing the different tasks required of the computer, could be stored inside the machine which did not have to be rewired to face each new task. The early valve-driven computer were soon programmed to prove theorems in logic and plane geometry, play checkers and chess, compose music and solve calculus problems (Armer, 1963, p. 396). Assuming that the human brain was "the most amazing computing machine ever devised" (Miller, Galanter and Pribram, 1960, p. 188) the new psychological scientists contended that human beings were not passive S-R mechanisms but active information-processing systems with a capacity for storing information in memory and retrieving it on cue. As Neisser (1967) remarked a little later, "A program . . . is a recipe for selecting, storing, recovering, combining, outputting and generally manipulating information" (Neisser, 1967, p. 8). Since people do this too, the computer simulation of human performance was seen to be a ready way to formulate a cognitive psychological science.

As a general rule, authors more interested in psychological functions than in computer programmes worried about the homunculus problem whereas their reverse counterparts did not. None of them paid any attention to the social conditions influencing behavior. For example, Miller, Galanter and Pribram (1960), in an early programmatic essay on computer simulation of human performance, pick a concept referring to any programmable string of events and tie it to other concepts. "A plan is any hierarchical process in the organism that can control the order in which a sequence of operations is to be performed" (Miller, Galanter and Pribram, 1960, p. 16). There are plans for remembering, forgetting, speaking, problem-solving, and so on. The famous TOTE unit is a feedback loop (servomechanism) which describes how plans are activated. Remarkably similar to the Piagetian psychological triad (assimilation, accommodation, and adaptation), it is said to transmit information, "energy" (for organic servomechanisms) and "control" (for guiding the execution of plans) (p. 26-28).

They try to deal with the "homunculus" problem by what largely amounts to a series of verbal hat-tricks. "Intention, " for example, is taken as referring to "the uncompleted parts of a Plan whose execution has already begun" (p. 61) and "effort of will" is "inner speech" or "inner shouting" which is "the Plan that is running our information-processing equipment" (p. 71). All this is backed by a quotation from a philosopher, C.I. Lewis, who adds a "homunculus" to their own concern with "knowing," "doing" and "valuing." "For a being," writes Lewis, "which did not assign comparative values, deliberate action would be pointless; and for one which did not know it would be impossible" (p. 71). To make one with Lewis and stiffen their homuncular edifice, they mention "self-made Plans" and add a special plea. "It is not too improbable, we feel, that consciousness is in some essential way the capacity to execute them" (p. 111). In this way they hope, the behavioural traffic can be initiated and sustained without the postulation ad infinitum of some further agency.

This problem is more effectively solved by someone more concerned with programmes than with people and with psychological functions. To Reitman (1965), for example, the "homunculus" is a control process built into programmes, nothing more. Since he tries to transform psychological functions so that they can be easily programmed, it is not surprising that he confuses a fact, computer simulation as a method of solving problems formerly solved by human beings (Reitman, 1965, pp. 3-4) with a hope, computer simulation as a way of understanding psychological functions (p. 2). In this circumstance it is also not surprising that his formulations of the latter project are not cogent. For example, "creative problem solving" is analysed by referring to the composition of a fugue by an unnamed (and possibly uncreative) musician. Reitman assumes that the composer has an "ill-defined problem," the solution to which is hampered by so many constraints (pp. 170-171) that the so-called "creative solution" amounts to transformations of the original problem into fresh restatements or ways of looking at it (p. 176). This solution is buttressed by some quotations: for example, "one may solve one's problems not only by getting what one wants but also by wanting what one gets" (p. 177), and "legislatures have been known to fit precinct boundaries to existing political concentrations as assiduously as . . . scientists sometimes fit curves describing lawful functions to concentrations of data points" (ibid.).

Occasionally this account of creative problem solving may be correct, but not always. Much more often the creative solution entails a break with the constraints of previous formulations and the establishment of new ones, posssibly with different constraints. Shakespeare went far beyond the old histories and plays on which his work was based. The natural sciences are replete with examples of an old theory, conventionally "patched" to meet anomalous findings, being gradually replaced by a novel one (Kuhn, 1964, p. 78).

Enamoured of computer-based, information-processing techniques as a way of representing "central processes," Reitman was forced into an artificial simplification of these processes. The contemporary range of minicomputers are increasingly doing many things formerly done by people, and this is usually acceptable to commercial enterprises which want to lay off slower and potentially troublesome human beings, but successful programmes may well be different from the functioning of their human counterparts. Indeed, Reitman lists Neisser's (1963) claim that human beings and programmes show certain fundamental differences: the former get bored, suffer from conflicts, have a memory system that is quite unlike that of a computer, a point recently made by Estes (1980), and generally grow and develop in a way programmes do not (Reitman, p. 18). To these could be added a social life, especially sexual liaisons, which might be difficult to represent on hardware.

Neisser (1967) himself, in his first attempt to relate cognitive functions to computer programmes, ignores all this and begins very much like Reitman. "The task of a psychologist trying to understand human cognition is analogous to that of a man trying to discover how a computer has been programmed" (Neisser, 1967, p. 6). And Neisser does indeed use the parallel vs sequential processing derived from his own "Pandemonium" recognition model. However, he formulates a cognitive theory by paying attention to lower-order peripheral processes (analysers) which synthesize and integrate information in a way reminiscent of pre-computer theories like that of Bartlett (1932).

> The central assertion is that seeing, hearing, and remembering are all acts of construction, which may make more or less use of stimulus information depending on circumstances. The constructive processes are assumed to have two stages, of which the first is fast, crude, wholistic, and parallel, while the second is deliberate, attentive, detailed, and sequential (p. 10).

Specifically, "Paying attention is not just analysing carefully; rather it is a constructive act" (p. 96).

The accuracy of this peripheral constructive activity has to be evaluated by "upstream" cognitive functions which operate like Bruner's (1951) "hypotheses testing." One makes a hypothesis about the original message, applies rules to determine what the input would be like if the hypothesis were true, and checks to see whether the input is really like that (pp. 193-194). This also resembles Dennett's (1978) concept of "generate and test."

There are two weaknesses about Neisser's account. The first is that his functions are isolated from each other, experimentally and by chapters in the book, without any recognition that the person is operating in a changing environment. For example, "visual cognition," "iconic storage," and "focal attention" are aspects of "pattern perception" and have only minimal hypothetical links with "auditory cognition," "echoic storage," and "auditory attention" which are features of speech perception. Bruner (1970a) the functionalist, describes this static weakness. "For mostly we search or recognize or image or think en route to carrying out some intended act, with the perceptual and cognitive routines subordinated to the achievement of some goal or objective" (Bruner, 1970a, p. 83). As will be noted, it is no accident that Neisser's work results in "an applied psychology of the dark room" (ibid). The second weakness of Neisser's constructionist and transformational psychology is his dealing with the homunculus problem in terms of an "executive routine" (p. 293) of the computer, a label which he is honest enough to admit does not deal with the behaviourists' charge.

Both weaknesses can be swept aside by accepting one of Simon's (1969) ideas concerning the design of artificial systems.

> In one way or another, the designer insulates the inner system from the environment, so that an invariant relation is maintained between inner system and goal, independent of variations over a wide range in most parameters that characterize the outer environment (Simon, 1969, p. 8).

For example, a change in the operations of a profit-maximizing business system can be predicted, if there is an alteration in sales-taxes, without any special knowledge of its decison-making apparatus. "The apparent complexity of human behavior over time is largely a reflection of the complexity of the environment in which he finds himself" (p. 25).

By using this concept in his later theory (Neisser, 1975; 1976) Neisser attempted to get rid of his twin bugbears, the homunculus and the environmental impact on cognitions. For example, the "schemata" for transforming, elaborating and storing information is replaced by Gibson's (1966) view that the function of the organism is to pick up the invariants of an ordered world in which the informaion is embedded.

> Perceptual learning is learning to extract the relevant information from the manifold available stimulation, that is, the invariant information that specifies the permanent layout of the environment, the distinctive features of things that populate and furnish the environment, and invariants of events that enable us to predict outcomes and detect causes (Gibson and Levin, 1975, p. 13).

In Neisser's own words, "ecological validity," a term borrowed from Brunswik (1957), is his target. "I believe that important aspects of the normal environment are being ignored in contemporary research paradigms. These aspects are the spatial, temporal, and intermodal continuities of real objects and events" (Neisser, 1976, p. 34), although he still uses cognition to refer to "the total of processes and activities by which people . . . acquire and use information" (Neisser, 1975, p. 159).

Reviewing his later book, Posner and McLean (1977, p. 482) generously interpret this to mean that Neisser is less interested in the processing mechanisms than in the external environment to which these schemata have become so flexibly adapted that its demand requirements give rise to them, although the two authors still prefer the 1967 theory. Another reviewer, Weimer (1977) is even more disenchanted with Neisser's book, pointing out that Gibson's postulation of information in the environment is just a guess and advancing his own theory of learning, based on a slightly altered form of Platonic idealism in which the potential for learning abstractions is innate (although changeable in a Lamarckian way). "Observation is not merely focussing one's attention on the data, but rather assimilation of the data into the conceptual scheme of the observer" (Weimer, 1977, p. 20).

Neisser faces an even more serious problem than this theoretical squabbling. Following Simon, he must assume that the invariant relationship is always with the physical environment, the carpentered world, and that, at least by implication, people can be insulated from variations in the social milieu which are sometimes unpredictable. For example, "the facts of cognition imply that the psychological manipulation of behavior is bound to fail" (Neisser, 1976, p. 177). This is at odds with the often-documented fact that cognitions can be readily manipulated by the agencies of mass persuasion which exist for this purpose (Cirino, 1971). J.F. Kennedy found that his popular appeal increased whenever he made a well-publicized speech attacking Communism (Hodgson, 1976, p. 45).

Again, Neisser says that "The prediction and control of behavior in the real world requires detailed knowledge of that world to a degree that we usually do not have, and that in any case falls outside the realm of psychological expertise" (p. 184). This places psychology right back in the lab and makes it a relatively useless discipline in the modern world (Bevan, 1976). It is ludicrous to accept quietly the idea that psychologists should know little about the "real world." Ye there are three reasons why this is the case. The first is the belief that cognitive psychology is a pure science, dealing with the acquisition, retrieval and use of information which can be used or misused by professionals in other fields for their own purposes (Neisser, 1975, p. 161), a position to be reviewed shortly. The second is that saying something about the real world can make psychology a dangerous trade for the person who wants to garner research grants from the funding agencies. The third is that learning for Neisser still is the perception of physical objects and events or their symbols.

This is all very well when applied to situations in which children find their way about a room or the transitive probabilities that characterize letter sequences in a language, but it is awkward when applied to social affairs where information is systematically rigged to maintain establishment ideas and profitable practices. Digging out and documenting the truth ("the permanent layout of the environment") requires a search of the more candid and unprofitable journals and small periodicals chronically short of funds, and from little read technical journals for bankers, industrialists, and so on. When this information has been retrieved, collated, and ordered into a coherent account, it will be read by almost nobody.

Consider the specific case of Exxon (Imperial Oil or Esso in Canada), the largest industrial company in the world. Originally a part of the old Rockefeller empire, Standard Oil of New Jersey, its executives have pursued a policy of control: of the oil supply in the non-communist world with the six other minor companies; of the prices for products; of political officials by bribery and corruption; and of information flowing to the man in the street and his less innocent political representatives. The last-named force is so powerful that a short-term *volte face* can be managed without fuss. In June, 1973, the Canadian Department of Energy, Mines and Resources, using figures supplied by the oil companies, predicted an eighty-year surplus of oil at reasonable prices. After the Arab-Israeli war of that year and the quadrupling of the price of oil, the companies warned that there would be a shortage of oil unless they were given adequate cash incentives to explore for new reserves. In October, 1974, the National Energy Board, again using (altered) data provided by the companies, reduced its estimates of oil reserves. "The eighty year surplus had become a seven and a half year surplus in the space of 16 months" (Laxer and Martin, 1976, p. 27). However, even after successive increases in the price of oil, Imperial's increased cash had gone into extracting the expensive oil from the Athabasca Tar Sands which will be sold at world prices. There is no incentive to explore further for "old gas, " particularly the sizeable amounts too expensive to recover in the old wells, until it too reaches world prices (Laxer and Martin, 1976, p. 33). By the middle of 1980, with the threat of an energy shortage coming on the heels of the political changes in Iran and its war with Iraq, that shortage had been widely advertised by the multinational oil companies together with the existence of hitherto unknown Canadian reserves to be exploited with the help of generous government aid.

In point of the flow of accurate information, this is an environment just as tightly-controlled as some mentioned by Neisser: "Tightly-controlled environments—prisoner-of-war camps, penal institutions, mental hospitals, and the like—often managed to control their inmates fairly well" (1976, p. 184). Admittedly the control of information is less salient and oppressive than the physical controls listed by Neisser, but it is equally effective in manipulating people to consume commodities and ideas unthinkingly, without considering alternatives (Ewen, 1976, p. 47). Accordingly, Neisser is quite wrong in his assertion that people cannot be manipulated under "ordinary cultural conditions" (1976, p. 177).

One can sympathize with Neisser's position. As a scientist, he must see that the real world is a place where strident expression is often given to controversial political and economic views. For example, consider Schiller's (1970) documented conclusion that

the modern mass communications perform a double service for their present-day controllers. At home, they help to overcome, by diversion in part, the lack of popular enthusiasm for the global role of imperial stewardship. Abroad, the antagonism to a renewed though less apparent colonial servitude has been quite successfully (to date) deflected and confused by the images and messages which originate in the United States but which flow continuously and through informational media (Schiller, 1970, p. 2).

Physicists, chemists, medical specialists and so on can ignore such dangerous remarks: why cannot psychologists as scientists adopt the same posture? The answer is that the behaviour of people in the real world is very much influenced by extra-laboratory political and economic events, suitably interpreted by the witting and unwitting agents of the status quo. The news from Bruner and Neisser that information is processed so that cognitive structures are established is neither very new nor very important. What *is* important is to arrive at an understanding of the goals of the major forces controlling them and the means by which they achieve that objective. Failure to do so means lack of recognition by the people who have to grapple with the events of everyday experience. For example, Heilbroner (1974) was surveying the future of man at the same time as Bandura (1974) was delivering a highly cognitive presidential speech in which he predicted fairly quick self-improvement with the help of psychologists. In his dismal scenario, Heilbroner used Lasswell's (1932, p. 30) contention that future authoritarian regimes would gain their legitimacy from people's latent tendency, stemming from their helplessness as children, to gain security by obeying authority. Lasswell's theory may be wrong, but Heilbroner's predictions have been more accurate than Bandura's. Indeed, it is usual for historians, economists, political scientists and other non-psychologists writing about human affairs to construct their own psychologies, paying no attention to professional psychological formulations (Silverman, 1977).

Unfortunately for Neisser, 1967 or 1975, the psychologist theorist and experimentalist must, if his aim is to gain attention as well as to build theories, deal with samples and variables which represent the real world of all of us who are faced with, to use a familiar phrase again, "the familiar priorities of power and money, set over against people." Boden (1977), unlike Neisser, attempts to do this without quite understanding the real nature of her task.

She believes that "Artificial Intelligence" (AI), computer programmes for illuminating "the principles of intelligence in general and human thought in particular" (1977, p. 5), can be used to counteract the "dehumanising influences of natural science" (ibid). Later, she contends in the same vein that "this area of deliberate artifice . . . bears on the most human concerns" (p. 393). This would seem to mean clarifying ideas because any computer programme must be unambiguously clear (p. 6), but at the same time Boden argues that AI programmes "can elucidate the essentially subjective mental realities so stressed by humanist psychologists . . ." and "the awesome complexity of the mind . . ." (p. 4). Understandably, her account of various AI programmes is characterized by claims and then their withdrawal or modification.

For example, she discusses an AI programme based on Freud's theory of neurosis, but admits that it parallels "actual neurosis" and the theory "only to a limited extent" (p. 21). This is not surprising because at each decision point—say which of the eight defence mechanisms to use against an anxiety-laden belief like "I hate father"—there is no decision-making agent to provide help. Instead, the author of the programme chooses to rank the defences "from low to high according to their effectiveness in reducing anxiety, and from high to low in respect of their effectiveness in providing discharge of the charge (cathexis) on each belief" (p. 28). A programme can be written to do this, but it is based on the author's assessment, possibly not particularly reliable, of the extent to which the various defence mechanisms fall along this dimension. Indeed the "objectivity" of the programmes is based on the criteria and assessments of the author. For example, the patient's statement "I hate father" might be made less threatening by the defence mechanism of denial expressed in "I will never abandon father" (p. 30). This is one opinion. The "denial" statement could be attributed to masochism or just plain habit exhibited by the patient or possibly the hating of the father might be less general than Boden imagines so that "I hate father" and "I must love father" (p. 25) are not as conflicting as the author presumes.

Similarly Abelson's *Ideology Machine*, based on his assumption that cognitive imbalance is uncomfortable and should be eradicated in favour of the more satisfying equilibrium, is influenced by the criteria and opinions accepted as correct by Abelson in his attempt to discover how a right-wing ideologue like Barry Goldwater would respond to certain questions (p. 69). It should also be noted, in passing, that the basic set of beliefs ("master scripts") attributed to Goldwater is uncommonly like those of both American parties at this particular time and that their assumption of a united "Free World" is less plausible than in Goldwater's heyday (Hoffman, 1980). Moreover, the problem of the *Ideology Machine* is that, unlike Goldwater and any other politician, it cannot deal with events in a context, especially unpredictable events. "Red China" was an enemy of the United States in Goldwater's time, but it is now a convenient ally. A computer model cannot allow for such changes over time and one can only assume that Abelson, like all computer simulators since Craik, was trying to use a technology that seemed to be more scientific than words to pin down that elusive entity, a science of cognitive psychology.

Boden eventually has also to face the obvious fact that computing science is at odds with, in her own phrase, ". . . meaningful action on the part of a subjective agent rather than a causal process in the natural world. Psychology must give an account of the meaning, or intentionality, intrinsic to mental life, and must recognise the wider theoretical implications of any such account" (pp. 395-396). To accomplish the feat of mixing this with AI, she discredits the former as a "science," thereby leaving AI as the only alternative "human science," a position with which only Dennett (1978) would agree.

For a start, she argues that these "humanist" psychologists have varied theories, none of which contains an explanation of the facts in question (p. 396), a point that could be applied to non-humanists. Again AI is described as "a technical language with which to discipline one's imagination" (p. 401) whereas "humanistic psychology" does not have the clarity of a scientific discipline of the AI type (p. 461). Finally, Boden finished off "humanistic psychology," and her own initial thesis, with the argument that, while AI programmes use psychological concepts and their work is within reach of the "idiosyncracy of peoples' world views . . ." (p. 457), nevertheless "detailed comparison of programs with human alternatives is at present hardly possible, because of our theoretical ignorance of human thought processes" (pp. 478-479).

This planting of inconsistent ideas in different places is seen to advantage when she deals with the "social significance" of "robots, " the first use of this term as a synonym of AI. She concludes that "robotisation confirms our insistence that we are essentially subjective creatures living through our own mental constructions of reality (among which science is one)" (p. 473). This conclusion is reached by a variety of arguments which centre on the commercial use of minicomputer programmes.

For example, the robots will improve the education of physicians, lawyers, teachers, and students by encouraging them to ask questions and pointing out their mistakes (pp. 448-449). As usual, this is more possible in scientific and technological disciplines than in other more controversial ones. Next, she takes on the complaints that robots would have a dehumanizing effect on people by pointing out that this condition already exists without robots and that, in any case, there is some evidence that neurotic patients prefer to deal with medical robots than with human psychiatrists whom they rarely get to see anyway (p. 457). People might also prefer to deal with "automatic lawyers, bureaucrats and teachers" (p. 458), and certainly domestic, industrial, and commercial robots would be useful.

However, there are problems not considered clearly enough by Boden. First, certain dissident ideas would reach even fewer people than they do now because home terminals would be linked on a two-way basis with a national network of computers to enable people to vote and express their opinions. She recognizes this possibility but argues that its effect would not be much worse than the "implicit and unquestioned assumptions" (p. 456) promoted by the more conventional, contemporary mass media. It would be much worse, however, because the criteria for evaluating the presence of dissidence and its justification could never be dealt with by AI programmes.

Second, robots would introduce "massive unemployment" which would have two beneficial effects. The drudgery of repetitive work would disappear, to be replaced by "varied, creative and autonomous work that is satisfying in itself . . ." (p. 462) and, presumably, so lucrative that unemployment would practically disappear. This "creative work" would be "the (currently) predominantly female welfare professions" (p. 462); moreover "men," from obsolete jobs, will take tutorial courses to "improve their minds" and so increase their interaction with other people that "we may therefore expect deep and wide-ranging changes in definitions of sexual roles" (pp. 462-463). Indeed, "men" will have to give up a commitment to the "Protestant ethic" which drives them to be providers for their families consisting of housewives in the kitchen and children in the schools.

In the contemporary world of high unemployment and high inflation, Boden's conclusion is fanciful. Women often work to help keep the family income at a satisfactory level. Work in welfare institutions is difficult for anyone to get, women as well as men. The "Protestant ethic" has been criticized as a motive for work (McCormack, 1969) and Boden is unacquainted with the literature still generated by the concept. Her assumption that the existing social order is static, and that "men" will just have to adjust themselves to its vagaries, prime among which is perennial unemployment, is an idea that makes even conservatives nervous. Any society which fails to provide work at adequate wage levels for the majority of its citizens will find that they do not wish to participate in its institutions or defense. At worst, it will be characterized by strikes, riots, and, if its military and paramilitary power weakens, by revolution in some form. Boden knows a great deal about AI, but very little about people and society. She is not alone in this: Evans (1979), another AI advocate, believes it will rid the world of Marxism.

Why deal with this line of research into the computer simulation of behaviour? There are two answers. First, if cognitive psychology was to be a psychological science, its best chance seemed to be in the hope of an adequate computer simulation of psychological functions. Always an unlikely possibility because people are often unstable, irrational, and much affected by the context in which they live, it has been a failure as complete as the theories whose authors dealt only in words, spatial concepts and inferences. Second, computer simulation, as a part of computing science, is associated with the momentum of a capitalism in which people have mattered little. Probably Hacker (1971, pp. 162-163) is right in arguing that this has always been the case, at all times and places. What is new in the last three decades, however, is the fact that ordinary people in Western societies have become aware, directly in their own lives and vicariously by watching television, of what relative "affluence" means and they are not about to give it up without a fight. It is sad to see psychologists slaving away at developing a basic cognitive theory of performance using computer terminology without paying attention to this sort of social context which clearly influences thoughts and behaviour.

The conclusion is that the computer simulation of a radical, or context-free, cognitive psychology cannot be part of any kind of science. Such scepticism is reinforced by more abstract considerations (Ehrenfeld, 1978, p. 159; Platt, 1966, p. 75). Even Dennett's attempt to close the gap between people and computers by arguing that neither really do experience pain (Dennett, 1978, pp. 221-224) has only a wild verbal splendour about it. On the other hand, dealing with memory, surely an entity or process that people share with computers, Estes (1980) has shown that human memory is quite different from computer memory partly in the speed of retrieval of items of information (Estes, pp. 63-64) and partly in the way the memory systems are organized. Human memory is ". . . oriented towards events and their attributes rather than toward the retention of items as units—forgetting is characteristically a progressive loss of precision of information about an event rather than a matter of total recall or total loss of a stored item" (p. 65). As Estes concludes, this sacrifice of accuracy of recall for a rough approximation is useful for human beings who must behave adaptively to variations in their environments (p. 67, p. 68). And there is the final contention by most natural scientists that AI programmes are not an explanation in the scientific sense.

3 / OVERTURES TO ORTHODOXY: CONVENTIONAL COGNITIVE THEORY

Since the main problem with computer simulation was its inability to deal with the social context, we must presume that software psychological theories are able to tackle this task more effectively. However, before we can evaluate the extent to which this is the case, a picture must be drawn of the society in which psychologists operate.

A. The Familiar Priorities

The industrial revolution had many social consequences, notable among which was a new class division based on money rather than status, and a correlated emphasis on economic growth as a desirable goal because it created jobs and improved the standard of living of just about everybody. Recently, it has been touted as the necessary economic basis for alleviating poverty and the plight of poorer regions. Few people, however, talk concretely about economic growth "for that would call into question the primacy of commercial interests and the profit system" (Gonick, 1971, p. 135). Let us consider, then, the experiences of people living in a society propelled by economic growth.

First, there is a proliferation of profitable consumer goods which largely ignores the common needs of the majority of people for housing, recreation, decent medical services, adequate public transportation and recreational, cultural and athletic facilities (p. 137). This economic situation, in which large, private, commercial interests (particularly oil companies nowadays) make considerable profits for their own benefit, is not an economic given, a reality. Nevertheless it is sold to the public as such because these interests own the mass media which promote the sale of goods and the soundness of the economic order based on material consumption. Offered no alternative or threatened by the horrible consequences of extreme existing alternatives, people, especially psychologists, work within the restrictions of the social order, giving and accepting private explanations of problems largely created by that order which is beyond examination (Drummond, 1978). The unstable economic nature of such an order is attributed by media forces to non-economic factors such as huge government bureaucracies which print too much paper money and limit the freedom of people to do more or less as they please. "What ails America," according to Meyer (1980) is that its "freedoms" are "entangled" in 80 years of "red tape," although it is clear that the regulations are designed to prevent people from experiencing the hazards associated with Meyer's libertarianism in an increasingly complex society. Who, it must be asked, has the liberty to do what to whom?

What Meyer does not reveal—and this is the second characteristic of societies burdened with growthmanship—is that the public sector of the economy controlled by governments has two components. The legitimate public sector deals with common needs (health, housing, employment) while its illegitimate counterpart provides unprofitable services and requirements that commercial and business interests do not want to underwrite—training scientists, technologists, and skilled workers, and building highways and airports without which the business community cannot function. Into the illegitimate sector goes the bailing out of failing private enterprises such as Chrysler and the occasional small bankrupt bank. Since actions in the public domain must be financed through the much-hated taxes and since the hidden illegitimate sector absorbs an increasing amount of tax revenues, the legitimate public sector is relatively deprived of funds and political friends. To describe this social imbalance Galbraith reserves his finer passages. "The family which takes its mauve and cerise, air-conditioned, power-steered, and power-braked automobile out for a tour passes through cities that are badly paved, made hideous by litter, blighted buildings, billboards..." (Galbraith, 1958, p. 199). Twenty years later, this imbalance still persists (Galbraith, 1975; 1980). In fact, in the contemporary economic recession combined with sizeable inflation, the call for a reduction in taxation has become much louder despite the fact that, after Japan, the United States is the most lightly-taxed developed country in the world (Newsweek, April 10, 1978, p. 10). Hacker's remarks, extreme ten years ago, now seem commonplace. "We have arrived at the point where we consider our liberties in dire jeopardy if tax notices compel us to forgo recarpeting our living rooms or to put off a vacation trip to London or Las Vegas" (Hacker, 1971, p. 132).

A growthmanship economy has other negative features: depletion of resources, waste disposal problems, an increase in noise, congested roads and environmental deterioration ("acid rain"), all of which are functionally related to poor physical health (Gonick, 1971, p. 146) and mental breakdowns (Drummond, 1977). The allegedly "good" growth alternatives (diesel fuel) to "bad" growth alternatives (unleaded gasoline) are also polluting (Rapoport, 1980. p. 64). Further automation will lead, together with tax cutting, to a considerable increase in unemployment which is the one single, very significant, correlate of mental ill-health (Drummond, 1977).

A psychological solution to this state of affairs is neither likely nor realistic. Lacking any strong radical tradition, North American society has shied away from the more appropriate economic and political remedies to a kind of flexible and powerful economic system that has a clear impact on people. As Levitt (1972) has remarked: "The ruthless commercialization of human relations in the name of growth, progress and efficiency obviously benefits the owners of the great corporations" (Levitt, 1972, p. 5) and Smith (1978) has suggested very tentatively that contemporary social conditions are a breeding ground for psychopaths. Hyman (1979) has noted that schools cannot be expected to tackle successfully the educational and social problems produced by "the present system of capitalism based purely on productivity and profit . . ." (Hyman, 1979, p. 1027). In this case what would be the nature of a cognitive psychological science?

In 1955 some important contributions to cognitive psychology were published or read. Psychometricians Meehl and Cronbach (1955, p. 281) argued that cognitions as hypothetical constructs had an influence on behavior that was not necessarily dependent on the environment, an idea available but not salient in the 1940s, and they coined the phrase "construct validity" to refer to the way in which the scientific status of an inferred variable could be determined by observing its correlations with other variables in the theoretical network (p. 293). And Miller (1955) pointed out that the limited "span of immediate memory" was the reason why people used rules to organize and reorganize apparently scattered pieces of information into the superordinate hierarchies so characteristic of human functioning. Examples include the Morse Code in which sounds are recoded into letters, then words, then phrases, then sentences, and the establishment of natural laws in algebraic terms which summarize many observations from different experiments (Miller, 1955, pp. 131-132). Language is also characterized by this form of superordination because of its redundancy and the consequent predictability of the message it carries: ". . . it does seem reasonable to assume that the hierarchical organisation of language—sounds or letters, syllables, words, phrases, clauses, sentences, paragraphs—is not an accidental pattern, but truly represents the preferred mode of operation of our mental machinery" (p. 134). Using communication in the seminal way, Miller concluded that scientific advances were a product of the "need for mental economy." "It is possible to think of many of the great advances in human thought as discoveries of more economical ways to package information that must be stored in the mnemonic warehouse" (p. 132).

In a paper delivered in 1955, Bruner (1957), Miller's associate, gave an attractive account of information processing that delighted the military men who were alarmed by the apparent technological supremacy of the Russians in the late 1950s. He was more of a pragmatic functionalist than Miller because he wanted to consolidate into a useful theory the interaction of learning, motivation and personality which produced "those active, adaptive functions of the organism which lead to the governance and control of all higher-order functions . . ." (in Anglin, 1974, p. 44). In the paper delivered at a symposium labelled Contemporary Approaches to Cognition and held at the University of Colorado, Bruner described his influential version of cognitive theory and wedded it, explicitly, to "creativity" and improved educational achievement. Wittingly or unwittingly, he had become for a few years the psychological scientist who supported the military buildup against Communist powers, particularly the Soviet Union.

B. Bruner and Consensus Ideas

Much more than Dewey, for whom he had great respect (in Anglin, 1974, p. 469), Bruner was a consensus man. He believed that youngsters in school could learn a great deal more if they had a more modern curriculum and teachers with a better knowledge of instructional theory (p. 478). The poor, labelled "underprivileged" by Bruner (p. 476) need not be handicapped in this acquisition of symbolic skills (pp. 466-467). Finally, psychologists were to be in the forefront of this new attempt to "amplify man's powers" (p. 479). This last claim is made with that elegant vagueness, the hallmark of someone who has never taught, which forestalls criticism.

Psychologists must re-enter the field of education in order to contribute to man's further evolution, an evolution that now proceeds through social invention. For it is psychology more than any other discipline that has the tools for exploring the limits of man's perfectibility. By doing so, it can, I think, have its major social impact by keeping lively the fullest sense of what is possible (p. 478).

Although this sounds silly nowadays, it was written by the man who threw in his lot with the Pentagon in the late 1950s and had no idea of the feeble impact American schools had on their students (Andreski, 1973, chap. 6).

C. Bruner and National Security

In 1957, Bruner's "higher-order functions" had become "codes," a set of abstract concepts which, he thought, should be the basis of disciplines (symbolic systems) taught in schools (Bruner, 1957, p. 65), of transfer of training and of "creativity." By 1963 he found that these codes were preformed by functional language frames so that, presumably their acquisition could be accelerated by suitable teaching (Bruner and Olver, 1963). This learning of functional codes (or cognitive structures) to be transmitted by the schools was most obviously reflected in the scientific and technological achievements essential for the industrialization and military security of any contemporary society. And so it was not surprising that Bruner was asked to summarize the proceedings of a conference called by the National Academy of Sciences to discuss the improvement of scientific education in schools. This Woods Hole Conference, attended by thirty-five scientists, scholars, and educators, was financed by the National Science Foundation, the U.S. Office of Education, the Air Force and the RAND corporation (Bruner, 1960, p. ix).

At this particular time, authorities in the United States were terrified at the military threat of the "missile gap" supposed to exist because of the successful launching of Sputnik, "a simple radio beeper in a ball of metal" (Kaiser, 1975, p. 494) in October, 1957. "For years afterwards ... it was widely believed in the West that the U.S.S.R had surpassed America in rocketry, space technology and related fields. This belief, shared by the American Congress, caused a radical change in American priorities involving tens of billions of dollars" (p. 494). This was the historical context of the Woods Hole Conference, on the basis of the proceedings of which Bruner wrote his successful *The Process of Education*. That he was well aware of the function of Woods Hole is shown by his concentration upon "national security." For example he states that the "gap" between physics taught in the school and that known to the physicists is "a gap of particular importance because of revolutionary advances in science and the crisis in national security" (p. 70). Again, "The Soviet Union's conquest in space, its capability of producing not only powerful weapons but also an effective industrial society, have shaken American complacency to a degree that looking back, would have seemed inconceivable a decade ago" (p. 75).

In the cause of bringing American industrial capability up to that of the Soviet Union by promoting the acquisition of "excellence" (especially in scientific and technological knowledge), Bruner advances ideas as to how these "fundamental structures" (p. 23) or codes can be taught more effectively to nearly everybody. These ideas need not detain us here partly because, like the "spiral curriculum," they are well-known, and partly because, by the late 1960s, a surplus of scientists had been produced without any evidence that Bruner was responsible for this state of affairs. What is significant is the fact that of all methods for improving educational performance, Bruner chose the one that was least controversial and expensive—changing curricula and teaching methods—and the one most likely to fail because the lowly-paid and lowly-esteemed teachers were almost certain to be the worst models for transmitting even the finest curriculum to their charges.

Significant too is Bruner's worry that his postulated drive for "excellence" may benefit only the gifted few, a "meritocracy"—Young's "The rise of the Meritocracy, " in which the term had been used in a pejorative sense, had appeared in 1958—leaving behind "the late bloomer, the early rebel, the child from the emotionally indifferent home ..." (p. 78). The facts are that the competition is for material advantages ("progress") and that the acquisition of Bruner's codes leading to such advantages is restricted to a small percentage of people. The reasons for this state of affairs—hereditary limitations or an impoverished background—are not worth arguing about because nothing can be done to alter either of them. The unproductive nature of such an enquiry was to be revealed a decade later when Jensen (1972, pp. 6-34) supported amid controversy the hereditarian viewpoint. Bruner, always the trimmer, was on the side of the American angels: he believed that performance on symbolic tasks was affected not by heredity but by poor teaching, about the improvement of which he offered familiar nostrums in an interview (Bruner, 1970b).

None of Bruner's ideas are new but they are expressed in a cheerful way which is greatly helped by the refusal of the interviewer to follow up pertinaciously some of Bruner's glib answers. According to Bruner, "Education is in a state of crisis" (Bruner, 1970b, p. 51) and he would like to see people do something about that crisis so that he can get on with "our science as usual" (ibid). The actions to be taken are, as before, curricular and private. For example, the spiral curriculum in which complex problem-solving stategies are taught in a simple form to a young child is given another airing (pp. 53, 54). Again, the problem of the poor environment is dodged by arguing that what counts is training the child to get as much as possible out of his environment by way of acquiring problem-solving skills. The high probability that children in a poor environment may never have parents with the capacity and time to "structure their children's environment in terms of problems to be solved (p. 56) is ignored. The notion that this idea should be applied to "bring the black into the system" (ibid) was shallow and unrealistic at a time when a recession and a decline in defense spending had resulted in the laying off of some highly qualified scientists and technologists. Bruner ends the interview on a Rousseauesque note by giving a hint of his findings about the brilliant learning skills of the young child, the implication being that these are undone by schools.

D. Bruner and the American Economic Empire

The goal of the American economic system was to persuade people regularly to buy commodities quickly made obsolete by poor manufacturing or by manipulated fashion changes (Gonick, 1971). This began to deplete easily accessible, local, non-renewable resources like oil, natural gas and aluminum so quickly that, in the early 1950s, presidential commissions began to report about the necessity for foreign investment in areas rich in these resources (Magdoff, 1969, pp. 80-82). Ways had to be found to exploit these resources to the advantage of the American empire but without irritating the natives whose customs and way of life were usually at odds with business interests. Arensberg and Niehoff (1964), in their *Introducing Social Change: A Manual for Americans Overseas*, argue that the way to do this is by providing formal schooling and technological training to the rising generation with expectations of future material rewards and status. "There are no people in the world who do not recognize the obvious utility of improved technological methods or devices" (Arensberg and Niehoff, 1964, p. 33). And again, "People do not borrow indiscriminately; they borrow what will best fit the pattern of their own culture and they favour technological changes over social and religious changes" (p. 63).

Bruner's (1966) assistance in this matter took the form of investigating the cultural influences (especially value orientation and language) on the acquisition by Woloff children in Africa and Inuit children in Alaska of the codes and functional abstractions which were the bases of technological advancement. Beginning with the relationship between value orientation and cognitive growth he constrasts "collective" (bad) and "individualistic" (good) orientations, defined respectively as a contrast between "social solidarity" and "individual coping." This distinction is illustrated from answers given to a conservation problem. Unschooled children (Woloff, European or American) could not answer the question, "Why do you say that this glass has more water than this one?" but could manage to respond to, "Why is thus and thus true?" (in Anglin, 1974, p. 372). From this information the following inference was drawn: "It would seem that the unschooled Woloff children lack Western self-consciousness; they do not distinguish between their own thought or statement about something and the thing itself. Thought and the object of thought seem to be one." (p. 372). Moreover, "it appears that school tends to give them (schooled Woloff children) something akin to Western self-consciousness . . ." (ibid) because they can distinguish between their cognitive functions and external events and classify the same stimuli "according to several different criteria or points of view" (p. 373).

At this point the hesitancy in Bruner's style should be noted. Although he is only at the beginning of his report, we find that modifiers are inserted into his account of the research findings: "could often," "would seem that," "seem to be," and, "It appears that schools tend to give" and so on. Similarly, phrases considered to be synonymous, like "different criteria or points of view" give the impression that Bruner is defensive about his positions, as well he may be, making large inferences about value-orientations from psychometric data. This brings us to a considerable difficulty, especially characteristic of cognitive theorizing, that militates against the status of psychology as a science. When a particular hypothesis is not corroborated, alterations are made in the theory so that the negative results do not appear quite so fatal as formerly (McGuire, 1973, p. 449). For example, "collective orientation" is equated with "realism" and is considered to be negatively related to "animism" or egocentricity characteristic of the "individualistic orientation" of Western societies. "We rather suspect it is only the powerful, well-cared-for competent child who sees the world in the pattern of his own feelings . . ." (p. 373). But the Eskimo children of Alaska perform in ways which run counter to Bruner's speculation. They are realistic, self-reliant, and achieve "superordinate structures" (codes) without going through a stage of egocentrism (animism) (pp. 373-373). To assimilate this anomaly, Bruner draws a distinction between "implicit egocentrism" or "unself-conscious realism" and "explicit egocentrism," arguing that the latter can be eradicated by allowing children to pour the liquid in the conservation experiments. Ignoring the results with Eskimo children, Bruner provides further evidence to the effect that the latter form of realism can be removed by "promoting an active manipulative approach to the physical world" (p. 375). Very pragmatic indeed.

In his conclusion, Bruner reverses this cause-and-effect relationship. "It may be that a collective, rather than an individual, value-orientation develops where the individual lacks power over the physical world" (p. 376). Although this runs afoul of the initial findings Bruner sticks to his original thesis: that an "individual orientation" or "Western self-consciousness" or explicit realism will occur in cultures in which the individual and his competence are valued as such, separate from, and independent of, any culture to which the person belongs. However, since a collective orientation (and individual powerlessness) is systematically encouraged in socialisation, it can be combatted by having the students actively participate in their own learning so that the Western emphasis on the individual and his "intentionality" is encouraged.

Bruner, despite his wriggling, never quite manages to establish this value orientation thesis; what he has shown is that conservation problems can be more quickly solved if children from a society with a collective orientation are allowed to manipulate the apparatus. Nowhere does Bruner demonstrate that these children, even when schooled, foreshadow the replacement of that collective orientation with an individualistic one which Bruner quietly prefers. We do know that a "collective orientation" can be destroyed if Western education is introduced with or without jobs that have no connection with the indigenous hunting, agricultural or gathering economy. Traditional native employment and adult authorities decline in importance and an "individualistic value orientation" begins to emerge independently of any "superordinate structures" (Preston, 1979). One would assume that, as the products of Western industrial society (including television) penetrate into the Arctic, South America, and Africa, any "collective orientation" will come under heavy pressure as people seek to acquire the material advantages available. This state of affairs can be reversed only if the group is walled off, usually from the larger individualistic society, the Hutterites being an obvious example (Peter, 1979).

Worth noting are Bruner's definitions of "individualism" as "individual coping" and "Western self-consciousness." Although this may look like trying to flog a dead linguistic horse, nevertheless it should be pointed out that these phrases are very ambiguous. A person with "individualism" may do a great deal more than merely "cope" with his milieu; people in Communist societies seem, by all accounts, to "cope" very well (Leys, 1978) and, in stringent circumstances requiring instant gratification and the removal of unpleasantness, they manage to survive as if they had "Western self-consciousness" (Feifer, 1980, p. 34). Moreover, there is the question of "individualism" with respect to what? Certainly, in point of social affairs, Americans are notorious for being conformist. Even de Tocqueville noticed this.

His study of the effect of language on cognitive growth looks to be more promising. His previous position (Bruner and Olver, 1963) was that the availability of superordinate words accelerates the acquisition of superordinate groupings. In the cross-cultural study, this is rephrased as follows: "the presence or absence of higher-order words . . . can be used to integrate different domains of words and objects into hierarchical structures" (p. 386). With cross-cultural data, he shows this relationship by noting the marked change from simple labelling and "pointing" in the case of unschooled Woloff children to the use of superordination in language and concepts by their grade 6 counterparts who were Woloff-French bilinguals or French monolinguals. This, he decides, is a product of the emphasis by the school on writing which "forces a remoteness of reference on the language uses..." (p. 388) so that the language becomes independent of its referents. The separation of words and their referents destroys verbal realism (the word is a real as the referent) and places the words in people's heads, an idea explicit in the works of both Miller and Craik.

But is the finding so unusual? Western countries (Britain, France, America) have been educating for a long time selected youngsters from underdeveloped countries (Nehru, Ho Chi Min, Yamani). If these countries want to become industrialized and militarized (as they always do), their leading cadres must learn at least one of the small number of universal (multinational) languages embedded in which are superordinate conceptual groupings. The case of the Eskimos is not inconsistent with this conclusion because surivial in their cold barren land requires an acquaintance with "cognitive maps" (spatial relations) useful for solving Piaget's conservation problems.

However, Bruner is not content with scoring merely one point. He wants to associate this intellectual realisation of hierarchial structures (words in people's heads) with his former concept of "individualistic value orientation." Accordingly, he argues that this separation of the individual means that "the individual must conceptually separate himself from the group; he must become self-conscious aware of having a particular slant on things, a certain individuality" (pp. 388-389).

This brings back all the old semantic problems of "individuality" together with the extensive Russian military and technological advances. Presumably, in the scientific domain the Russian inventor has "a particular slant on things" which does not transfer to social affairs. Bruner's obvious tactic is to let go of his concept of "value orienation"; unfortunately he does not do this until he is satisfied that he has accomplished what he has set out to prove.

E. Bruner and Instructional Technology

During the Second World War it had been discovered that the principles of learning (practice, meaningfulness, feedback as information, reinforcement, and so on) had "limited applicability" (Smith and Smith, 1966, p. 172) to the problems of teaching people to use military equipment. In this applied setting, as Gagne (1962a) had indicated, the principles of learning took the form of specific task analysis into subsidiary components so that there would be intra-task transfer of the learning of component parts to facilitate the total learning of the task (Gagne, 1962a, p. 28). The training media, which aided the person to learn the final task included simulators and "concept trainers" (predating Skinner's teaching machines), were especially useful in identifying subordinate tasks and sequencing them "to insure maximal positive transfer to the final task" (Smith and Smith, 1966, p. 90).

Although it is clear from the accounts of Gagne and Smith and Smith that each task required different skills, those reported by Gagne ranging from sensory-motor skill to a knowledge of electronics, nevertheless Gagne (1962a, p. 86) is clearly uneasy about the difference between learning principles from high-status academic laboratory research and those from low-status military training. In the 1962 edition of his *The Conditions of Learning*, he had attempted to combine the two by establishing a hierarchy of common modes of learning, ranging from simple associations to problem solving and their curriculum correlates, across different disciplines. In the 1977 edition, this hierarchy is described in different terms as running from "basic forms of learning of the simple associative sort" to an "information-processing model of learning." Most important of all, however, the different disciplines are arranged under five apparently psychological skills: "intellectual skills," "cognitive skills," "cognitive strategies," "verbal information," "motor skills," and "attitudes," within each of which the learning begins with the simple basic associative form and ends with information processing of some sort.

Gagne's hierarchies have been dogged with two sorts of troubles. First, the relationship between the subordinate and the supraordinate performance is sometimes described in logical, sometimes in empirical and probabilistic terms. An example of the latter is, "A learning hierarchy, then, identifies a set of intellectual skills that are ordered in a manner indicating substantial amounts of positive transfer from those skills of lower positions to connected ones of higher position" (1962b, p. 239). This is clearly a question to be settled by empirical investigation, possibly carried out by a psychologist with an interest in mathematics. However, occasionally the hierarchical hypothesis is buttressed by an appeal to logic: "our hypothesis was that . . . no individual could perform the final task without having these subordinate capabilities . . ." (p. 356). Gagne's (1973, p. 207) hierarchies in mathematics are usually developed by using the latter condition of logical incorporation of the sub-skills into the higher-ordered skills. It is pointless to substantiate empirically such a hierarchy (Phillips and Kelly, 1975, p. 361).

Moreover, although White (1973. p. 155) had found that Gagne's intellectual skills are difficult to identify outside mathematics, Gagne (1974) and White and Gagne (1974) have softened White's criticism in two ways. First, they accept White's point that learning hierarchies are most effective in quantitative skills in which the hierarchy contains only a few elements (White and Gagne, 1974, pp. 21-22). although it is speculated that they may widely "exist across subject areas" (p. 23). Second, an attempt is made to dissociate Gagne from Ausubel's very similar thesis of subsumption on the grounds that the latter is concerned with the learning of verbal information (p. 26) whereas Gagne's sub-skills deal with the information-processing psychological part of learning (Gagne, 1974, p. 13). The distinction once again, is between the "content" of the instruction and the "internal conditions of learning" (p. 14). Such a distinction is not cogent. Even the findings let him down. Specifically, White and Gagne (p. 21) report that preschool children cannot understand the meaning of "greater than" and "less than" until they grasp the meaning of "equals." It is difficult to see how this is anything more than a performance skill which may be generalized to other disciplines with similar content.

Disregarding White, what Gagne did in 1977 was to describe subordinate-superordinate relationships ambiguously in terms that could be construed as logical or empirical. Examples include "the vector relation of forces" which is said to be resolved into "prerequisite components" (p. 144) and "judging equalities and inequalities of liquid volumes in rectangular containers" whose "subordinate concepts need" to be learned first (p. 157). Of course, some subordinate skills must be learned before superordinate ones, but this learning is not necessarily of a logical hierarchy even in quantitative skills. Gagne simply asserts that the subordinate skills are "the only essential previously learned skills that the child must be able to recall in undertaking the learning of a new intellectual skill" (p. 274). Moreover, as is implied in White's work, certain disciplines, notably the humane and social studies (and even motor performance based on modeling) do not lend themselves to analysis in terms of hierarchical procedures. And finally, if the relationships are of a logical sort, then the learning must be domain-specific and based on a knowledge of the skills in question. In this case, the equipotentiality principle—that the study of any kind of learning will yield principles that transfer to all kinds of learning—is invalid and the psychologist becomes an endangered species.

Bruner was influenced by Gagne, but had no intention of allowing his "coding" to be bogged down in such problems which he simply bypassed. For him, intellectual growth became the learning of "internalized culturally transmitted technologies" (Greenfield, 1966, p. 226) for representing the world in terms of action, imagery and finally, abstract symbols (Bruner, 1966a, p. 6). He laid down for such a theory some prescriptive features, salient among which is the following:

> a theory of instruction must specify the ways in which a body of knowledge should be structured so that it can most readily be grasped by the learner . . . a theory of instruction should specify the most effective sequences in which to present the materials to be learned. Given, for example, that one wishes to teach the structure of modern physical theory, how does one proceed? (1966b, p. 44).

Why should Bruner meddle in instructional theory which, a decade later, was still very programmatic (Glaser, 1976; 1982)? One answer is that, as Gagne reported, it had been successful in military training. Perhaps a more important reason was its consistency with American values like progress and equality of educational opportunity that were a buttress to the Head Start Program which had just begun in 1965. The contention was that most students can and should master what the school provides, regardless of the limits of home environment and the more putative ones of genetical heritage.

In his defence of instructional theory, Bruner contends that, as far as symbolic activity is concerned, man has emerged from Darwin's evolutionary sequence by using tools, language and other symbols to acquire a pool of knowledge which, transmitted by education, means that every organism need not acquire information and codes anew by self-discovery. Sometimes (in Anglin, 1974, p. 326) he asserts further that man's use of tools enlarged his brain, and sometimes he reverts to the more Darwinian position that the brain must develop slowly to the point where the people with larger brains survived because they could use the tools (p. 327). In any case, "We move, perceive, and think in a fashion that depends upon techniques rather than upon wired-in arrangement in our nervous system" (ibid.). These "tools," sensory-motor, perceptual, and abstract, are "external resources" (Bruner, 1966a, p. 26) which—and this is implied by his continuous refusal to discuss individual differences—just about everyone could use to become educated and prosperous. Factors like poor teachers, slums, parental hostility to the school, are not considered impediments to the acquisition of the economic and powerful codes which represent for Bruner the most attractive way to achieve an education.

The discussion of an impoverished environment and all the anti-educational features it entails can be avoided in two correlated ways; by stressing the importance of "intrinsic motivation" and by blaming teachers for the substandard performance of youngsters. Accordingly, Bruner states that "cognitive growth or intellectual mastery is rewarding" (p. 30) and he blames the school for subverting the child's "intrinsic motive to learn":

> ... what the school imposes often fails to enlist the natural energies that sustain spontaneous learning ... curiosity, a desire for competence, aspiration to emulate a model, and a deep-sensed commitment to the web of social reciprocity (p. 127).

These are captivating assertions unsupported by any evidence. Doubtless an "intrinsic motive to learn" characterizes the behaviour of some people, but only an unrepresentative few (Kline, 1974). Moreover, the "web of reciprocity" is simply a bold speculation which is consistent with the notion of a biologically-based reciprocal altruism being bandied about at Harvard at this time (Trivers, 1971). In the contemporary world, the existence of small wars, strikes, guerilla activity, racial riots and the threat of nuclear wars make the concept ridiculous and its exposition before psychologists by Campbell (1975) has received a well-deserved drubbing (Wispe and Thompson, 1976). At this time, Bruner was stringing together some foggy ideas that represent nothing.

> The corpus of learning ... is reciprocal. A culture ... is a set of values, skills, and ways of life that no one member of society masters. Knowledge in this sense is like a rope, each strand of which extends no more than a few inches along its whole length, all being intertwined to give a solidity to the whole. The conduct of our educational system has been curiously blind to this interdependent nature of knowledge (p. 126).

This is merely a moving around of words to induce hopefulness and reduce regret; it is certainly not discursive prose dealing with events or behavior referents. If, that is, psychologists are not allowed to grapple with reality in a certain domain, then they will deal with—indeed be encouraged to deal with—fantasy. A more detailed account of this idea will appear later.

Again, although Bruner is predominantly concerned with coding in the disciplines that were important at the time, mathematics, science, and technology (pp. 33, 35, 52), nevertheless he does return to a more complete description and analysis of his 1965 report, "Man: a course of study," with its emphasis on the nature of man (the inner man) rather than on the aspects of society which form and influence behaviour. This is a sanitized approach since the nature of American society in the middle 1960s was far from pleasant (Baran and Sweezy, 1966, Chap. 10; Galbraith, 1967) and the reason for this condition, the momentum of the post-industrial capitalism and its emphasis on the importance of getting and spending, was not a topic that a funded researcher like Bruner would want to touch. Instead, he considers questions like "What is human about human beings? How did they get that way? How can they be made more so?" (p. 74). Changing man, and this was Dewey's (1916, p. 24) way, means making him more "human," i.e., developing his potential—presumably for acquiring codes. The five "great humanizing forces" are tool-making, language, social organization (the "web of reciprocity" again), education and "man's urge to explain the world" (p. 75). These "forces" are dealt with in a curiously formal way, quite unlike the substantial culture impact they must have on each society.

For example, language is treated as a means of communication (p. 77), grammar and syntax are to be taught by using games (pp. 78-79), and "the universal characteristics of all human languages" (p. 80) is a part of the course. A very formal account is given of how language "shapes characteristics and thought" (ibid., p. 80). Yet, this last point is surely the most important, far more important than grammar and syntax and the supposed "universal characteristics of human language." Very soon-and there is no need to be radical to take this stance-the ruling ideas and feelings of any society must be got into the heads of its youngsters, even those who are very young. Toynbee (1967) has made this point in prose that cannot be summarized.

> Every stable society imposes on the majority of its members the social and economic beneficiaries. A corollary to this law ... is that a society is constantly evolving a new language of automatic self-justification (Toynbee, 1967, p. 95).

Toynbee offers as an example, the meaning of "public expenditure," an appropriate term in the contemporary world of Proposition 13 (Blaustein, 1979) and a resurrected Milton Friedman. Toynbee defines the term as a phrase which instantly evokes shocked disapproval, and a vision of tea-swilling bureaucrats proliferating in public offices. But what the Rich mean by their constant demand that public expenditure should be reduced is ... that less money should be spent on the Poor" (p. 98). And much more on military hardware. Clearly a funded researcher could not afford such candor.

The same point can be made of "tool making" in which a picture is drawn of hominids running around with sticks and stones. No mention is made of contemporary sophisticated technology in warfare or industry which results in the "powerlessness" disliked by Bruner (1970a, p. 56). Similarly, social organization is described in terms of social structure "marked by reciprocity and exchange," and of families, all dealt with very abstractly (pp. 84-86). Interactions of social classes—say a common person's encounter with a physician, a lawyer, a stockbroker, or a car dealer—are not dealt with in the context of "reciprocity and exchange." In these "exchanges" as Hapgood (1974) points out, the common person gives a great deal more than he ever receives in return.

"Child rearing" in the "Course of Study" treats the "mastery of skill for its own sake" (p. 86) and the "shaping of man by the patterning of his childhood" (p. 87). Again, nothing is specified. What skill, for example? Some are very anti-social. More, is it to be childhood in a slum or in a very rich family? And prediction of this "shaping" is very poor indeed (Clarke and Clarke, 1976).

"World view," purporting to describe "how particular human societies express their human capacities" (p. 87), mentions two primitive hunting-gathering societies (p. 90). But no attention is paid to the demeaning of these "human capacities" in contemporary industrial societies: the automating of craft skills (Braverman, 1974); the increase in numbers of people living in poverty, or even in starvation (George, 1978); and the depersonalizing effects of existing in prisons (Abbott, 1980) and mental homes (Rosenhan, 1973). Not surprisingly, social studies are to be simulated in games or the activities of the Netsilik Eskimoes; well away, that is, from "the familiar priorities of power and money, set over against people" (Williams, 1968, p. 13), of which we have made much mention.

F. Bruner and Values

In his 1966 collection of essays, Bruner (1966b) accepts the fact that educational systems must produce "technicians and engineers and scientists because we are living in a world of accelerating technology" (p. 33), but he also voices concern that some "wise social policy" must be taught . . . again in schools . . . before people with these technocratic skills succeed in destroying the planet (p. 23). This caution became more dominant in 1971 when Bruner (1971b) was replacing his emphasis on teaching of symbolic structures with one on values.

I would be quite satisfied with a de-emphasis on the structure of knowledge. . . . If I had my choice now, in terms of a curriculum project of the '70s' it would be to find a means whereby we could bring society back to its sense of values and priorities in life. I believe I would be quite satisfied to declare, if not a moratorium, then something of a de-emphasis on matters that had to do with the structure of history, the structure of physics, the nature of mathematical consistency, and deal with it rather in the context of the problems that face us (1977b, pp. 20-21).

The most outstanding problems were the continuation of a seemingly unpopular war, student dissidence (especially at Harvard in 1969 when Bruner saw the police turned loose on the students), the economic recession of 1969 combined mysteriously with an upsurge of inflation, and the environmental and population issues raised in a popular form by Ehrlich

(1968). In fact Bruner never carried out a research programme of this sort. In any case it could never have been accomplished without reference to the nature of the society in which he lived, its historical context and the low probability that schools would be effective in this area (Anderson, 1979).

Indeed, Bruner was a standard "pure" psychologist who thought that his plausible cognitive theory had implications for educational practice. This mistake has been discussed by Ebel (1967). Moreover, his theory was not original; from Miller he took the notion of hierarchies and of the limit to information-processing set by memory; from Piaget came the general idea of development and the tests of abstraction, and from Vygotsky the idea that superordinate groupings (hierarchies) were associated with functional language frames. He used these themes—and other current ones—as a source of educational improvement, at home and abroad and regardless of social conditions. He patched vigorously his hypotheses to surmount negative results and, as has been noted, he was unaware of the non-academic tradition in American public schools (Collins, 1980). Still, the Great Society promised in the middle 1960s had to be promoted by somebody, and Bruner took the bait.

G. Piaget Emerges

Piaget, as a cognitive and developmental theorist, was largely ignored until the late 1950s. In Britain, where his early texts were published in the 1920s and 1930s, he was never a force to be reckoned with partly because of the strong attack by Victoria Hazlitt (1930) and partly because he decided beforehand what intellectual (logical) operations would appear at certain ages—concrete operations like logic of classes and the logic of class relations, seriation, the conservation of amount and the development of hierarchies at 7+, to be followed by the conservation of weight and volume and, at 11+, the combinatorial structure of binary positions, and the four groups freely borrowed from algebra. Again, he merely illustrated these logical operations, labelled functions to give them the nuance of behaviour, and made no attempt to study the effect of teaching on them. More, the entire corpus of his work was subject to the usual criticism of circular reasoning (Brainerd, 1977, p. 936) and his attempt to circumvent this procedure by arguing that he was dealing with "process" is conceptually and empirically false (Jensen, 1972, p. 78). There were also weaknesses in his theory, particularly the license given by the concept of "horizontal decalage" to explain away negative results (Brown and Desforges, 1977, p. 9; Wason and Johnson-Laird, 1972, p. 190), and its restricted applicability to mathematics and the natural sciences (Piaget, 1972).

From the point of view of the practical teacher the theory was unrealistic: the average adolescent could never find an answer to the simple logical problems, let alone those requiring a knowledge of symbolic logic for their successful solution. Piaget's counters were that if this were the case in certain symbolic domains, it might not be in others (horizontal decalage) or that the students had not been properly taught in the sense that their solutions arrived at by outmoded methods (assimilation) should have been corrected by suitable apparatus and teacher preparation (accommodation) until a correct solution had been achieved (adaption). In theory this strategy was consistent with the self-discovery method advocated by Dewey and Plowden (in Nyquist and Hawes, 1972, pp. 11-12), but it bore no semblance of reality to the usual classroom situation. The ratio of its cost-benefit analysis was too high and any putatively successful implementation would have required a brilliant and dedicated (and well-paid) group of teachers.

Why, then, did Piaget's theory conquer the social intellectuals in the United States when his book with Inhelder, *The Growth of Logical Thinking from Childhood to Adolescence* (1958), was published in an English translation? Various mutually compatible reasons can be given: it was timely (after Sputnik) and new to the members of the "redeemer society" on the lookout for conceptual progress without institutional change; it came with a handy variety of tests which made research easy, and, most important of all, it gave scientists, mathematicians and industrialists support for a "new mathematics" curriculum designed to stimulate the production of scientists and technologists (Bruner, 1960, pp. 43-46). It was widely—and wrongly—assumed that such a curriculum had been responsible for Russian technological advances (Froome, 1970, pp. 107-108), and some vested interests in the 1950s were keen to introduce into the high school pieces of the university curriculum (Kline, 1974, p. 25). Indeed, Inhelder (and Bruner) contended that this process, in a simple form, could be extended into the primary school. All in all, there was money in the business of studying Piaget's operations, especially in attempts to accelerate the child's understanding of them. The possibility that any such acceleration might have only a temporary value, unrelated to later learning, was ignored in the euphoria of finding a new, hopeful theory of child development, funding for the study of which was easily available.

Forgotten was the fact that Hazlitt (1930) had made three important criticisms of Piaget which have been corroborated independently now that the enthusiasm for him is waning. The first concerns semantic issues. When the presence of a Piagetian stage is being detected, the language of the items has to be selected carefully so that the inability of the child to comprehend should not be attributed to adult language, unfamiliar to the child, in which the test item is phrased. Hazlitt (1930, p. 354) noted that Piaget's view of preconceptual egocentricity, in which relations of various sorts are misconceived, could be attributed to his use of words not normally used by the children. Support of her position is drawn from a casual reporting of results derived from the performance of an unspecified number of children. In one study, for example, in which the problem is one of making an exception—something the average preconceptual child cannot do, according to Piaget—she found that the children could not use "except" spontaneously but they could solve the problem practically, especially if "except" were replaced by the phrase "but not." "Is it legitimate," Hazlitt asks, "to assume that the whole core of thinking lies in being able to attach the given process to the word 'except' rather than to any equivalent that the child may prefer?" (p. 356). After replicating the findings using pictures (p. 357), Hazlitt concludes that the use and understanding of words comes much earlier than the processes to which they refer, a point to be rediscovered and used more systematically by Vygotsky (1962).

Later writers have also raised semantic issues when dealing with Piaget. Wilson (1972) questions Piaget's attribution of ideas to children without appropriate evidence. For example, the famous experiment on the conservation of liquid finds Piaget arguing that the children between four and six years of age "... think that the liquid increases or decreases in quantity..." (p. 18) because of the greater or lesser height of the new glasses as compared to the standard original glass from which it was poured. Wilson wonders whether the children think that the liquid increases. When they say, "there's more in the (new) glass," could not this mean "higher"? After all where would they think "more," in the sense of "something added," came from? Again do they reason, as Piaget imputes to them, that there is "more" in the new glass because the glass is higher, i.e., do they use height as a reason? (pp. 18-19). Finally, Piaget argues that since the child "is perfectly well aware of the transformation" of liquid from the standard glass to the taller glass, how can he not see it as a "reversible movement"? As Wilson asks, "Is he aware of it as a 'transformation,' or is it to him a process of growth or increase?" (p. 19).

The problem is Piaget's usual emphasis on logic rather more than on experience, and his consequent bias in the interpretation of the children's answers to his protocols. Phillips and Kelly (1975) point to his contention that there are some concepts at the beginning of the stage of concrete operations which cannot be derived from experience. And yet empirically, the understanding of the conservation of substance is a prerequisite for that of the conservation of weight and volume, although the reverse seems to be the case from Piaget's protocols. And Phillips and Kelly quote from a 1972 paper by Piaget to the following effect:

> What is a constant and invariant substance when it doesn't yet have a constant weight or a constant volume. No experiment no experience, can show the child that there is the same amount of substance.... He knows that something is conserved but he doesn't know what. It is not yet the weight, it is not yet the volume; it is simply a logical form—a logical necessity (p. 370).

The basis of this claim is the famous study in which a ball of plasticene is rolled into a sausage shape from a standard shape, and the child is asked whether it has the same amount of material, the same weight, and the same volume as it had before. At about eight the child conserves amount; later weight is conserved, and then still later volume. The argument for the priority of substance is based on the remark by the eight-year-olds that "there is the same amount of plasticene." Piaget reasons that, since plasticene is an amount of substance, then substance must be conserved before weight and volume. However, as Phillips and Kelly remark, the children are conserving the amount of plasticene, not of an abstract "substance": "... perhaps the children believed that the same amount of plasticene was present because they knew that none had either been removed or added" (ibid.).

Hazlitt's second criticism deals with the assumption that teachers could get the child to understand, say, the concepts of weight and volume at a much earlier age than Piaget plumped for if these topics were of any interest or value to the child (Hazlitt, 1931, p. 360). This idea has recently been exploited by Brainerd (1977) in his attack on Piaget's notion of stages of development which control how and when learning processes operate. As Brainerd is well aware, cognitive development in Piaget's theory is a series of successive and invariant stages, each of which is controlled by an appropriate set of cognitive (logical) structures. At each stage, learning is the successful application of the available structures to new content. If these structures are appropriate, then learning takes place; this process is labelled assimilation, a term Piaget borrowed from biology. If they are inappropriate, then learning cannot take place until the structures are altered until they are more stage-appropriate to fit the content; this is Piaget's accomodation, a term with Darwinian implications. Intellectual development, then—and the term is synonymous with American terms like "growth" and "progress"—presupposes sequences of assimilation and accomodation which enable children to remove themselves progressively from a slavish dependence on the environment so that their performance becomes less determined by stimuli immediately impinging on it. This approach has advantages: it has a scientific flavour; it is desirably "progressive" and far removed from the mechanism and determinism of Hull and Skinner; it is quite consistent with Zener's (1937) demonstration that as soon as sub-human organisms are freed from the constraints of the apparatus or the experimental situation, their behaviour is quite different from that previously observed. The weakness of the Piagetian approach lies in its postulation of an invariant sequence of stages of cognitive development, each stage consisting of correlated logical operations (*structure d'ensembles*) and being related, in an admittedly flexible way, to chronological age.

Consider conservation problems as an example. These begin with stimuli that are equivalent with respect to some property (number, length, mass, volume and so on). This equivalence is apparently destroyed by some visible transformation and the subject is questioned as to whether he or she has conserved the quantitative identity. Piaget believes that the development of conservation is characterized by three stages. Stage I is preoperational and the child does not possess the structures for understanding conservation; in Stage III the child is in command of concrete operations which will allow him to understand conservation and, in transitional Stage II, the child possesses a mixture of intuitive, preoperational and concrete grouping structures and is in a state of "cognitive disequilibrium." If Piaget's theory of learning is correct, training will make transitional children learn to solve conservational problems to a significantly greater degree than preoperational children. As Brainerd (pp. 922-924) points out, in the pretest stage children were placed in the three stages in terms of their performance and Stage III subjects were discarded. Experimental and control groups were established and various treatments (reinforcement, verbal rule instruction, conflict procedure) were administered to the former groups. After training, a battery of posttests, usually the same as the pretests, was administered and an estimate of the improvement in performance of experimental Stage I and Stage II groups established. For all of the researchers reviewed, Stage II children were clearly superior to those in Stage I.

Brainerd is unhappy with this relationship between pretest and posttest scores as an estimate of what subjects know because, as he shows, test reliability will make this relationship positive even when the true relationship is zero or negative (p. 925). Accordingly, he turns to difference scores between pretest and posttest performance for Stage I and Stage II subjects (pp. 926-927), and finds no evidence that the latter group learned more than the former, i.e., that "children's susceptibility to conservation training is closely related to their pretraining stage classification" (p. 929). This is true also of concepts other than conservation: seriation, classification and spatial concepts (pp. 934-935). A second problem concerning Brainerd is the Piagetian assumption that, since preoperational children do not possess the structures required for conservation, they could gain no lasting benefit from conservation training. Studies with children who failed the number conservation test and with preoperational children showed that this was not so. Although the gains were smaller with preschoolers, nevertheless these subjects showed the characteristics observed in the case of older children—susceptibility to a variety of training methods, transfer of learning to types of conservation not used for training and retention of learning across intervals of a week or more training (p. 933).

Hazlitt's final criticism of Piaget's heavily logical developmental process is that common adults unfamiliar with the material make the same mistakes as children. Dealing with Piaget's description of how children at the early concrete stage of development explained the displacement of objects of different size and density either by giving the weight or the size "without bringing the two into relation in giving different causes for the same phenomenon" (Hazlitt, p. 361), Hazlitt reports, without giving any data, that her "non-scientific adults" showed the same responses and she draws the following conclusion: "Piaget's picture of a striking difference between adult and childish thinking is, I believe, due to an over-valuation of verbal expression as a measure of thinking, and an exaggerated view of the logicality of adult thought" (ibid.). Evidence about the latter point has been provided by Odom (1978, pp. 122-123 and reported by Desforges and Brown, 1979, p. 279).

What is being maintained here is that attainment in a discipline is determined much more by the context and previous experience in that discipline than by, say, any "cognitive level" the learner may somehow have reached. One example of this is a simple experiment by Wason and Johnson-Laird (1972) in which they placed four cards, on each of which appeared one of the four symbols E, K, 4, 7, in front of "highly-intelligent subjects" and gave them the following instructions. "If a card has a vowel on one side, then it has an even number on the other side. Your task is to name those cards, and only those cards, which need to be turned over in order to determine whether the rule is true or false." The rule, it should be noted, referred only to those four cards.

The problem can be treated logically by putting p for E, not -p for K, q for 4 and not -q for 7. As Wason and Johnson-Laird argue, "the correct course of action . . . is to attempt to falsify the rule. . . . It is necessary to select p to ensure that no value, other than q, occurs with it. . . . This (also) requires the subject to select not -q (because p occurring with it would falsify) . . ." (pp. 174-175). The correct answer, p and not -q, was discovered by a distressingly small number of people, even after a variety of authors had gone to considerable lengths to make it easy for their subjects, university students. In fact, in four different experiments, only five out of 128 (less than four percent) of subjects got their initial selection correct (p. 182), a finding at apparent odds with Piaget's contention that the adolescent ". . . is capable of thinking in terms of propositions which take account of the possible and the hypothetical. He will be able to isolate the variables in a problem and subject them to a combinatorial analysis which nicely exhausts the possibilities" (p. 189). "But this," as Wason and Johnson-Laird conclude, "of course, is exactly what most of our subjects conspicuously fail to do" (ibid.).

They conclude that formal operations are only elicited by familiar tasks, and not cognitive skills which can be applied to any problem whatsoever. Piaget (1972) himself, seems to have moved toward a similar position; and just prior to his death apparently admitted that his stage-dependent theory was probably mistaken (Golinkoff, 1982). In other words, they are really practical rules rather than formal operation. That is, they are matters more properly the concern of logicians and mathematicians in theory, and of discipline specialists in practice. Most people, even educated professionals, reason poorly outside the domain of their interests and professional skills partly because they learned to reason in that domain and partly because reasoning is rarely important and emphasized in social life and leisure pursuits. This conclusion has been supported and extended by Brown and Desforges (1977, p. 15). Unfortunately the study of learning (the skill) has been conventionally allocated to psychologists; the problem of learning *what* (the content) has been for long ignored because it was considered the psychological science would develop units of explanation and laws of behaviour that would be applicable to all sorts of disciplines and domains. Few people nowadays have such a sanguine view of this affair, although the psychologist as special educator may provide some diagnostic and teaching help at the most elementary levels. Apart from that, however, the learning of mathematics is a matter for the mathematician or psychologist who has some undergraduate training in mathematics. For example, Traub (1965), following Gagne (1962b), speaks of analyzing a task into a set of subtasks, "all logically necessary for the performance of the task" (p. 54). The task turned out to be the graphical addition of positive and negative integers, and Traub discovered that students working on heterogeneous subtask problems, defined as such in mathematical terms, performed the task better than those who worked on homogeneous or other problems. He speculates that this is caused by the greater amount of information contained in the former problems (p. 50) but, since the information is specific to a subject-matter domain, it is difficult to see where the psychologist enters the picture. Shayer (1979, p. 271) has given some life to the Piagetian psychologist by reporting fresh data supporting a unitary factor of "formal operational thinking," but Desforges and Brown (1979) point out that this explains nothing: it could be a product of individual differences in IQ or science teaching or a combination of both. In any case it is irrelevant to the main problem of how to design and teach a science curriculum in the usual classroom.

Why did the Bruner-Piaget line of research turn out to be so fruitless? The prime reason is that the authors failed to distinguish between what is properly the domain of psychology (person perception, personality, psychotherapy, motivation, social psychology) and that of academic disciplines like mathematics. For example, a term like "coding" can be used in any psychological domain or in a neutral one like rat running or letter sequences in a language, but it should be turned over to professionals in a domain in which it is embedded. It is significant that there is no plausible application of the two authors' ideas beyond mathematics and the natural sciences and that, when Bruner studied transfer of training in mathematics, he was assisted by a small army of mathematicians (in Anglin, 1974, Chap. 24).

In other words, the hopes of the young Thorndike and his supporters have been dashed; there is no body of scientific psychology which can be used to improve every aspect of schooling, especially the teaching of school disciplines which was much better carried out before systematic psychology began to appear (Eurich and Kraetsch, 1982; Jones, 1981). On the other hand, fragments of psychological theory (cognitive ideas) have usually stayed well within the psychological domain, and to their fate we now turn.

4 / OVERTURES TO ORTHODOXY: COGNITIVE IDEAS

Formerly, when so-called scientific theories of performance were being described, complaints were made partly about their claim to scientific status and partly about their inability to deal with aspects of society which influence that performance. Now, however, when concepts or fragments of a theory purporting to have social significance are being considered, the more pressing necessity is for psychologists to tackle the social problems, to which the likely solutions are economic and political. Like any well-bred social scientist, cognitive psychologists devised concepts to support the existing social system (the Risky Shift, the Need for Entrepreneurial Achievement, the Inner Person, the Identity Crisis), especially when it began to crumble (Values Clarification). For example, during the economic stagnation after the Korean war, businessmen needed backing for their mystique about the "free-market economy" which offered material advantages because of a ready supply of hard-working people with entrepreneurial ambition and a willingness to take risks, and who had a good chance of rising to financial success by means of their own unrestricted efforts (Galbraith, 1958, p. 56). More accurate information to the effect that this pseudo-competitive system of corporate capitalism was abridged by monopolies, by labour unions, legislation and so on (p. 43) and was substantially supported from the public purse, was anathema, even to workers (Lane, 1967, p. 265). The executives of large corporations were also very touchy about the remarks made about them by Whyte (1956, p. 226) in *The Organization Man*, who expressed and documented the idea that, as Cartwright (1973, p. 223) puts it, "groups, by demanding conformity to norms, tended to stifle creativity, innovation and the unwillingness to take risks." Despite the fact that this was not an unusual thesis to psychologists (Asch, 1954) and that the scope of executives' operations and their access to resources and rewards could not be accurately represented in a laboratory or testing setting, some psychologists stood by to defend the system with handy conceptual weaponry. The "risky shift," "need for achievement" and other "inner person" concepts illustrate the character of this arsenal.

A. The Risky Shift

The Choice Dilemmas Questionnaire (CDQ) was used to measure risk-taking in individuals after an unpublished pilot investigation in 1961. The usual experimental design involved repeated measures; the CDQ was given to individuals who were then formed into a group and asked to arrive at an unanimous "group" answer to each item. In contrast to Whyte's stance, the groups turned out to be significantly more willing to take a risk than individuals, and the shift in mean scores from the individual to the group condition was labelled the "risky shift." For almost 10 years a profitable "line of research" developed around this topic with its readily-available test and research procedures (Cartwright, pp. 223-224).

The initial finding was heartening. According to received opinion, the businessman as entrepreneur justified himself because he took risks that, say, a civil servant did not. Only now has it become widely known to the interested amateur that the large corporations, the heartland of the economic system in Western developing countries, prefer a government to pay as much as possible of the cost of risky ventures, leaving them in the enviable position of having risk-free profits guaranteed (Pratt, 1976, p. 24). However, in the 1950s, this idea was completely hidden from many professionals, especially psychologists whose training in experimental design was a massive (and welcome) shield against the then dangerous trade of making statements about the real world of business manoeuvres.

There were further reasons why a line of research began to develop in this area. (a) The findings were replicated, regardless of the sex and occupational status of the group; (b) they were consistent with the opinions of the members of the liberal consensus who favoured "inner-directedness" and "intrinsic motivation" as against "social conformity" and "extrinsic motivation"; (c) a research procedure and a test were available so that researchers did not require to spend time in the awkward, and often fruitless, task of test construction, and (d) the name "risky shift" appeared to have affinities with the "red shift" known to astronomers who were very hard scientists indeed. Admittedly the "risky shift" departed from the astronomical concept by generating about a dozen different explanations to which their proponents, in true psychological fashion, clung tenaciously, but this has the added advantage of generating more research (Cartwright, 1973, pp. 224-225). In the long run, however, the large number of findings and the absence of any stable thesis called into question the nature of the risky shift and the psychometric value of its dominant measuring instrument, the CDQ.

Two problems appeared after the first flush of enthusiasm and stable results. The first centered on the test itself, consisting of 12 items each of which asked the respondent to select the lowest probability of success that would justify the course of action described in the item. The summed or averaged probabilities gave the CDQ score, the assumption being that the smaller probabilities reflected a greater risk-taking disposition. Item-analysis led to the following disquieting conclusions. (a) Although item shifts were stable across environmental settings, the direction and magnitude of the shifts were different for the different items, most items showing little or no shifts. (b) Accordingly, CDQ items were constructed which led to "conservative shifts" and investigators using such items concluded that groups were more "conservative" or cautious than individuals. Second, other researchers using more natural risk-taking situations—those faced by investor, juries and consumers and those posing dilemmas involving the taking of ethical risks—reported inconsistent findings, a fact which underlines the possibility that the various meanings of the terms "risk" had been ignored by authors who relied on the accessible CDQ (Cartwright, 1973, p. 226).

Why did this now defunct line of enquiry last for 10 years, despite the fact that the original replicated findings were at odds with the early work of Asch, and the more contemporary findings of Milgram (1965) about obedience to authority? Cartwright offers three reasons. First, the label "risky shift" made the concept of risk-taking an attribute of individuals, steering it away from equally appropriate domains such as group problem-solving, group decision-making, social influences or attitudes in which the power of the group or the other person is more clearly discernible. Again, during the early years, research was carried out with the CDQ, a global measure of risk-taking, to the detriment of the setting (domain) and of behaviour in applied fields. Total score on this test became the primary dependent variable. No attempt was made to concentrate on performance in items, even when this was reported and when factorial designs were employed to study the effect of conditions on this global disposition, supposedly measured by the CDQ (p. 229). Third, the remarkable stability of the findings was impressive: this positive information was useful because it could be made the subject of research, lectures and even a chapter in Brown's 1965 book on *Social Psychology*.

Finally, Cartwright believes that critical attacks on the risky shift were deflected by the policy of editors who relayed papers containing these attacks for evaluation to "experts" already committed to the test and the research method usually employed. This delayed the appearance of documents questioning the conceptual and methodological assumptions of the previous work (p. 229). Meanwhile the important applied question as to whether an individual or a group should make decisions—medical, military, legal, and commercial and so on—was not asked, let alone made the subject of research. Cartwright argues that even applied research might not have "made a greater contribution to our understanding of the nature of group decisions involving risk" (p. 231). Perhaps so. After all, the original 1961 unpublished work was a master's thesis in business management at M.I.T. The decisions the author must have addressed himself to were of the corporate sort and their nature could not to be studied realistically by the laity.

B. The Need for Entrepreneurial Achievement

Another most convenient concept sponsored by McClelland in the early 1950s, served the same purpose as the "risky shift." In *The Achievement Motive*, published by McClelland and his associates in 1953, the "need for entrepreneurial achievement" (later it became the plainer "need for achievement"), was supposed to be measured by performance on projective tests, usually the interpretation of stories written about four (or more) Thematic Apperception Test cards. Even when the standard rules for scoring each story are adhered to, the results have been disappointing. After an extensive survey of the literature on the fantasy-based measure, Entwhistle (1972) concludes that the inconsistent results from various studies stem from the low reliability and predictive validity of the measure (Entwhistle, 1972, p. 390), that any correlations between fantasy-based measures of achievement and school performance can be accounted for by their joint relationship with verbal facility and IQ. Moreover, Entwhistle suggests that even this litany of unsatisfactory results may be misleading because of, as Cartwright noted, the "often remarked tendency of American editors to publish only positive findings . . ." (p. 385). And there is always the circularity problem, never addressed, together with the poor psychometric practice of using rating scales of unknown quality. These errors are revealed in a quick summary of some of McClelland's work.

In 1961 he produced *The Achieving Society*, consisting of researches carried out during the mild recession of the middle and late Eisenhower years which were characterized by the natural stagnation of a monopoly capitalism unaided by extensive public spending. McClelland, however, was concerned about two psychological ideas related to industrial productivity. The first was that "a society with a generally high level of achievement will produce more energetic entrepreneurs who, in turn, produce more rapid economic development" (1961, p. 205). More important factors such as the level of investment in any country and access to material resources were not mentioned by McClelland. The second idea was that the source of this need for entrepreneurial achievement was a stress by parents on independence, self-reliance and mastery-training for the child. Boys with high scores on need for achievement

> were encouraged to master something, and once they had done so, hold to it by restrictions against 'regressive' behaviour. The mothers of the 'lows', on the other hand, make more restrictions altogether, and do not expect their sons to show independence and mastery so early. In a word, their sons remain more dependent on adults, both for achievement, help and for restrictions, for a longer period of time (p. 342).

The latter idea, based on a slight piece of research, is now ignored; however, the general notion of trying to find mother-child relationships which are related to adult behaviour, now also under attack (Clarke and Clarke, 1976; Skolnick, 1978), was too useful to be abandoned by McClelland.

Two more ideas were added which helped to bring his theory into line with what he believes to be future entrepreneurial performance by an individual. The first was that encouraging "other directedness" in the child, possibly by some form of group play, would make him sensitive to the needs of others (pp. 402-403). That is, the entrepreneur must be on the lookout for these profitable needs. The second idea took care of the resemblance between "other directedness" and Whyte's "conformity"; "egocentricity" was added to the features of the potential achieving entrepreneur because he must take risks in conditions of moderate uncertainty in which his skills are likely to make a difference: "the overconfidence of the man with high achievement is based on his conviction that he can modify the outcome of an uncertain situation by his own personal achievement" (p. 224). This, not profit, is the spur; profit, rate of growth and so on are simply concrete feedback which signal success (p. 231). Accordingly, an individuals's motive for achievement may find pleasurable expression in working for a group. "A man may get achievement satisfaction from having contributed to a successful outcome and he therefore has some way of telling how well he has done" (p. 230). Hence the profit motive is replaced by the intrinsic (non-monetary) need for achievement and the business man is cleansed of his concern for filthy lucre.

There are many different sorts of problems here. The risk in any ventures involving corporate transactions is usually taken over by the public treasury (the exception is the small business man but he is not part of the heartland of an industrial economy); "other directedness" and "egocentricity" sit poorly together as characteristics of high achievers; the percentage of "high" and "low achievers" is never listed, although it must differ from sample to sample; as usual, the sampling problem is ignored and McClelland shows a handy talent for interpreting anomalous findings so that they fit his hypotheses. These and other criticisms of research into achievement motivation can be found in conventional studies (Maehr and Sjogren, 1971; Weiner, 1972). What is undeniable is the futility of trying to assess the motivation of corporate executives (or that of aspirants to that status) by the use of paper-and-pencil tests. Private companies do not address themselves to groups and their concerns but to the marketing of profitable commodities which, by means of advertising, they persuade individuals to buy. Oil companies are exclusively interested in their profits and not at all in providing cheap fuel to motorists, a point which became evident in 1974 when they successfully raised prices markedly in the face of proclaimed shortages (Asbell, 1976). The fact that corporate executives do not resemble McClelland's entrepreneurs (Galbraith, 1967, p. 129) does not mean that they are unconcerned about company profits in which they usually have a personal stake (Milliband, 1969, pp. 219-220). And, as has been noticed, these profits are made in situations of little risk, not of moderate uncertainty, as McClelland would have us believe. The fact that McClelland, compared to an intelligent layman, is poorly informed about the corporate world stems from his desire to derive appropriate behavioral laws about that world from a "pure" set of researches using variables that bear no relation to the real world of corporate functioning. Accordingly, the value of his work can lie only in its support of the advertized fantasies of the economic system.

The general attractiveness of McClelland lay in his explicit acceptance of the idea labelled "personal causation" by De Charms and Muir (1978, p. 92) and almost holy writ in the folklore of capitalism. If, that is, some people are at an economic disadvantage in society (poor health, living in slums, no hope of future advance), then it is their own fault because they are not sufficiently motivated to "shape their own destiny" (Loye, 1977, p. 437). This very private reason for a country's productivity is given at the expense of larger and more obvious factors: a decline in access to resources, the presence of destructive wars, increasing technological backwardness resulting in uncompetitively-priced products and a decline in investment in a world of floating currencies and rapidly-depleting non-renewable resources. If psychologists feel that they have something to contribute to an understanding of aspects of society beyond the laboratory and university domains, then they should become familiar with these aspects and their controlling forces. Psychologists who sally forth unarmed into this larger area usually make fools of themselves. For example, when dealing with his need for power, McClelland (1975) prophesied that there could be a "morally justified" war in the 1970s in which the United States would support the Arabs who "can shut off our oil supply" (McClelland, 1975, p. 365). Apart from the fact that the Arab states are very varied, some of the more feudal and conservative ones being strong supporters of the United States (Hottinger, 1980), the difficulty presented by OPEC is not an oil embargo but price increases, inevitable over time because of the decline in the value of the dollar and in the amount of non-renewable oil resources.

To be funded, people using cognitive ideas need not directly support the sentiments bruited abroad by the representatives of large economic forces. Equally helpful ideas may take the form of an emphasis on people's "potential" or "personal causation" of some sort, to the exclusion of any concern with the social context. A sample of these concepts is discussed below.

C. The Inner Person

Clearly if social changes are to be brought about in a society with unchanged major institutions, then it must be assumed that the impetus for, and sustenance of, that change will come from changed individuals. This notion was a main ingredient in the cognitive theory which sustained the outlook of the members of the liberal consensus. "The core assumption in internalism is that the critical determinants of human behavior lie within the individual" (Mahoney, 1977, pp. 5-6). The emphasis on the "inner person" took a variety of forms, some of which—the disreputable "creativity" line of research (Vernon, 1973)—require no mention, but others still linger on despite being besieged by incompatible findings and weak instrumentation, many tests being devised without any attempt to establish the fact that they are measuring the same thing (Gilmor, 1978, p. 8). For example, Rotter's (1966) I-E scale was advertised originally as differentiating between "internals" and "externals"; the former believed that reinforcements were contingent upon their own behaviour whereas the latter believed the rein-forcements were the result of luck or chance or powerful outside forces or unpredictable events. In a popular article, Rotter (1971) makes clear the value-laden nature of his dichotomy.

> Clearly we need continuing study to reverse this trend (toward externality). Our society has so many critical problems that it desperately needs as many active, participating internal-minded members as possible. If feelings of external control, alienation, and powerlessness continue to grow, we may be heading for a society of dropouts—each person sitting back, watching the world go by (p. 59).

Some criticisms of this stance are in order. (a) A sizeable percentage of people live in a society *into* which they would like to drop by getting a job (Adams et al., 1971, pp. 21-23; Heilbroner, 1976). (b) "Externality" has always had a bad press, although Rotter's argument could be countered with the assertions that, suitably led, "externals" would be just as productive as "internals" and that feelings of "alienation" are much more likely to be felt by intellectuals than by anybody else. However, from performance on the home-made scales, the disproportionate contribution of "externals" to "maladaptive behavior" is high. Examples listed by Gilmore (1978) include: frequency of smoking among ninth-grade females; incidence of premarital pregnancy among middle-class whites; antisocial behaviour by high school students and "drinking for reasons that related to personal problems rather than for enjoyment" (p. 9). These findings, apparently so distressing, come from simple univariate correlations which preclude the possibility that the "maladaptive behaviors" have multivariate causes and that partial correlation—or its equivalent, analysis of covariance—might eliminate most of the findings. (c) The average person realizes that his chance of controlling large events (economic policy, foreign policy) is much lower than that of controlling personal events. Thus, Gurin, Gurin, Lao and Beattie (1969), after analyzing the 23 items of Rotter's scale, found two orthogonal factors labelled "Control ideology" (the large events) and "Personal control ideology" (the small events). The dismal features of this state of affairs are that any distribution of test scores must be determined in large part by the "internality" or "externality" of the items, about the meaning of which there is considerable ambiguity (Janzen and Beeken, 1973, pp. 299-300), and that even items referring to events "within my personal control" have been at best, of limited predictive value (pp. 297-298).

Average, uninformed people know that they "feel free" only in very limited domains like a choice of available foods at meal times; they also know that in larger domains like acquiring and retaining a job, their personal power is almost non-existent in a corporate economic system which regards them exclusively as sources of profit rather than human beings with common needs. Since it is more profitable to hire (and fire if need be) an unskilled man than a skilled man, it is inevitable that the skill will be broken down into sub-skills and routine tasks which can be handled by mechanical processes attended by unskilled operatives whose number and cost must be smaller than the number and cost of the skilled men formerly employed (Braverman, 1974, pp 79-80). Accordingly, most jobs are of a menial repetitive sort and require only on-the-job training (p. 431). Moreover, when organized labour becomes an impediment to the maximization of profit by forcing up wages, the larger multinational corporations will transfer plant and capital to low-wage countries controlled by indigenous dictators (Laxer and Laxer, 1977, p. 61).

In this case, even the personal freedoms under the rubric of "personal control ideology" are limited almost exclusively to the individual's identification with the happenings and dominant figures of the fantasy industry. He can become one with them as they destroy the tyrannical forces of evil, or corrupt authority. Kerr (1977, p. 52) believes that such good and evil melodramas appeared on the stage in England in the troubled 1790s and were taken over by the movies to be transformed into "westerns" or police shows. It is much less dangerous to watch Clint Eastwood than to organize or participate in social action against authorities responsible for poor housing, unemployment, and other effects of an engineered recession which hits minority groups and the poor the hardest.

Clearly it is unrealistic for psychologists as scientists to bolster, wittingly or unwittingly, an established political and economic order which, by its very nature, creates the human problems the psychologist takes it upon himself to solve. For example, there is nothing he can do about the fact that most people without talents in a high-technology society are finding it increasingly difficult, during an economic depression when interest rates are high, to afford the material conveniences they formerly enjoyed and which are still displayed on television. There is little point in attributing this failure to a lack of need for achievement, poor vocational guidance (especially when there are no jobs), an unwillingness to take risks or a lack of intrinsic motivation. Human problems often arise from non-human forces beyond psychological control. Any attempt to ignore this insurmountable barrier will merely lead to queries about the status of psychology as a science. It is one thing to present arguments in support of a society; it is an altogether different matter to claim that they have a scientific status.

D. Freedom

Since freedom appears to be synonymous with "inner control," writers who specialize in "locus of control" have attempted to write about "freedom," a favorite idea in Western societies and not to be lightly dismissed since Western dissidents are not subject to the usual degradations from which their counterparts in totalitarian societies suffer. Consider the original meaning of the term: as a result of technological advancements in some countries during the eighteenth and nineteenth centuries, people were freed from the bonds of the totalitarian feudal system to "choose their religion, their pattern of life, their marriage partners, their occupations. They offered their services, their products, their savings, or their labour, on the market and got the market price . . ." (Macpherson, 1965, p. 6). For the masses with no capital and few skills, this price was usually only enough to keep them alive in a condition of miserable squalor described by the young Engels (Marcus, 1976) and by many other writers later in the nineteenth century (Pyke, 1967). Most people had been freed from feudal serfdom to live in penury and self-serving greediness, a point not lost on the young Marx (in Bottomore, 1963, p. 26).

To avoid the philosophical problem of the question, "freedom to do what?," and of the behaviouristic position, exemplified by Skinner (1972), that man is a slave of the environment, Lefcourt (1973) defines "freedom" as an "illusion," a belief, with certain observable consequences. Briefly, "The reported aversive quality of a stimulus decreases when subjects exercise control over that stimulus" (Lefcourt, 1973, p. 419). For example, subjects who administered electric shocks to themselves could tolerate higher levels of shock than subjects who suffered passively from shocks that were not under their control. However, the former group placed in the same position as the latter, became so intolerant of much lower levels of shock that they performed at the same level as the latter group. The findings from infra-human organisms are similar: dogs and rats with prior experience of escapable shock in a confined situation behaved more purposively and energetically in a later situation of escapable or inescapable shock than did their counterparts with no such previous experience (p. 423).

After describing these differences in terms of the relative amount of "perceived control" and "hope" on the part of the subjects, Lefcourt is rash enough to quote Mowrer as seeing some social implications in these researches. "Perhaps we have isolated here, in prototype, one of the central reasons why human beings so universally prize freedom and why threats to freedom, under a totalitarian regime, are anxiety-producing" (p. 420). This may have appeared a good guess to Mowrer in the late 1940s when he was preparing his 1950 book in which these comments appear, but it is less compelling now. "Threats to freedom" are not "anxiety-producing" to everybody in a totalitarian society, only to dissidents, a small percentage of the population. Stalin has returned to favour in the U.S.S.R. because he was a strong ruler and his bloodthirsty totalitarian rule was never experienced by ordinary people (Kaiser, 1976). Moreover, their Western counterparts who control only minor practical matters in everyday life (what to eat for breakfast, what car to buy, if you have the money, and so on) define themselves in terms of these areas (they are enthusiasts about sports, entertainment of all sorts and other leisure-time activities) and do not emphasize or regard as important situations over which they have no control—or, in Lefcourt's terms, they do not "perceive" themselves as having any control. Still, it must be pleasant for the ruling interests to find an experimentalist backing "freedom" and a "free society" without mentioning that it is more circumscribed than people believe and that it carries penalties which people suffer only when they try to exercise that freedom in supporting controversial political and economic ideas (Horowitz, 1962, pp. 33, 52-53, 57). Admittedly in certain countries dissident ideas may be expressed, but only in crisis-ridden, small-circulation periodicals read by those already converted.

E. Identity

It has always been very difficult for people moving from Nazi Germany to the more tolerant society of the United States, relatively affluent during the 1940s and 1950s, to be critical of their new homeland and realistic towards its apparent enemies. This striving to please was very strong when the newcomer was, like Erik Erikson,

> patently a friend of man. His emphasis falls on the altruistic strivings of youth, the satisfaction of motherhood, the wisdom and dignity of age, the indispensability of the nuclear family, and the need for harmony among the nations, which will surely outgrow their diversiveness (Crews, 1976, p. 9).

Indeed he eliminated the unpleasant emphasis on sex and death by Freud without going to the anarchistic extremes of Reich (in Elkind, 1971).

His "eight stages of man," the early ones partly based on Freud, from birth to 50 years, have positive poles with an optimistic moral quality about them—trust, autonomy, initiative, industry, identity, intimacy, generativity, ego-integrity—which must attract people, even although they are vaguely defined and have no obvious contact with the real world. This applies somewhat more to his famous thought-cliche, "identity," which refers to the person and the group. In the former sense, "identity" becomes a successful mastery of each stage of development, but in no deviant way. In Erikson's (1959) spongy prose, "The growing child must, at every step, derive a vitalizing sense from the awareness that his individual way of mastering experience is a successful variant of the way other people around him master experience and recognize such experience (Erikson, 1959, p. 89). Like every other thought cliche, this is appropriately ambiguous.

What is, then, the "American group identity"? Erikson tries to describe it in "Reflections on the American Identity," a chapter in his 1950 book, *Childhood and Society.*

> It (the American family) breeds, on the whole undogmatic people, ready to drive a bargain and then to compromise. It makes complete irresponsibility as impossible as it makes open hate and warfare in families. It also makes it quite impossible for the American adolescent to become what his brothers and sisters in other large countries becomes so easily, uncompromising ideologists. Nobody can be sure he is right, but everybody must compromise . . . for the sake of his future chance (1950, pp. 276-277).

This wishful thinking is Erikson's version of Bell's (1962) "end of ideology," and it comes as no surprise when he draws a parallel between this undogmatic character and the absence in the United States of any two-party system of the European sort. Community is wanted, not the divisiveness of class barriers (p. 278).

However, Erikson's consorting during the 1940s with writers doing "mainstream research" into "national character," culture and personality and so on, sponsored by RAND, the Office of Naval Research, and the Air Force (Crews, p. 13) has not put him completely out of touch with a superficial reading of American social history. He realizes that the adolescent's adaptability makes him vulnerable to "bosses" whom he regards as "a danger to the American identity" (p. 281). The "boss" is a self-made aristocrat who "enters boldly into the vacuum left by the emancipated sons in their endeavour to restrict themselves in fairness to others. He looks for areas where the law has been deliberately uncharted . . . and tries to use it and abuse it for his own purposes" (ibid.). Gutmann (1974, p. 61) believes that this is a prophecy of a future Watergate, but it was in fact a characteristic of American society. Originally party bosses as patrons functioned like feudal lords to the immigrants who could provide votes to a machine in return for help and guidance (Wills, 1970, p. 465). At the present time the bosses have been replaced by various "interest" or "issue" groups (Hodgson, 1980, chap. 5) whose effect is the same—and, administratively, much more inconvenient.

Despite "bossism," American youngsters achieve an "identity" which is described in terms of "national character." The adolescent boy is "tall, often taller than their fathers . . ." (Erikson, 1950, p. 272); the older sister is "slim, trim and poised . . ." (p. 279) and "these young truly are the backbone of the nation . . . in war or in peace, the fruit of American education is to be found in a combination of native mechanical ability, managerial autonomy, personalized leadership, and unobtrusive tolerance" (p. 280). It is reassuring for Erikson to believe that the "identity" of the Russians and Germans is rigid and that they must be convinced that "their protestantism is ours and ours, theirs" (p. 358).

It is difficult to know what to make of these passages beyond saying that they partake of the more serious information that goes into popular, mainly women's, magazines. They speak to popular fantasies and wish fulfillments, and the fact that only now is Erikson under professional criticism (Phillips and Kelly, 1975) and disappearing from textbooks is an indication that his writing was an attractive counterbalance to the more obviously uglier features of contemporary society in which, as is inevitable in the unregenerate economic system tolerated in the United States, people approximate to things that make profitable goods and services (Heron, 1979; Jacoby, 1975, p. 105). Non-renewable resources are rapidly being exhausted and, if Lasch (1979, pp. 17-18) is right, a narcissistic pessimism has replaced the public confidence that infected Erikson.

His most famous book, one in which "identity" is negatively related to a political attitude, is Young Man Luther, published in 1960 and subtitled A Study of Psychoanalysis in History. There, "ideology" is declared to be simplistic left-wing thinking which is a product of regression by individuals to infantile stages of development. It is seen as—and Erikson's passage is worth quoting—

referring to totalitarian systems of thought which distort historical truth by methods ranging from fanatic self-deception to shrewd falsification and cold propaganda . . . the total perspective created by ideological simplification reveals the strength by the dominance it exerts on the seeming logic of historical events, and by its influence on the identity formation of individuals (and thus on their "ego-strength") (Erikson, 1960, pp. 19-20).

Accordingly, Luther is described, not as Freud's anal character, but in Erikson's egoequivalent term "defiance" (p. 58) which explains his opposition to his father, his teachers and the Pope (p. 119). Unsurprisingly, Luther has an "identity crisis" characterized by an "inner split between the temptation to surrender and the need to dominate" (p. 152). Erikson goes on to claim, at least to his own satisfaction, that Luther moves through the later stages of development, intimacy, generativity (he got married and sired a child) and "integrity," the achievement of "authenticity" by the destruction of "existential anxiety" (pp. 254-257).

This contention cannot be taken seriously. There is no dismissal of alternative, non-psychoanalytic explanations because the relevant documents from Luther's time are scant in number and subject to quite different interpretations from those preferred by Erikson (Bainton, 1961, pp. 450-453). Despite the ambiguity of the term "identity," particularly in Erikson's hands, it exercised a fatal claim on the attention of psychologists during the 1950s and 1960s. Marcia (1966), for example, defines it in two different ways in the space of a few paragraphs; first, people have identity when they can find a niche for themselves in society and "maintain a feeling of continuity within themselves" (Marcia, 1966, p. 551). Later, identity is taken to mean a commitment, after some consideration of alternatives, to one occupation, and to an "ideology" after a reevaluation of "past beliefs" (pp. 551-552). Marcia also refers to Erikson's "moratorium" in which people defer commitments until they have made a decision, presumably one that is suitable for them and their society. "Foreclosure" refers to commitments being made before the "crisis" of indecision; Marcia presumes that the existence of "foreclosure" means that youngsters have followed their parents' wishes and that, therefore, in later life, they become authoritarian and conventional as measured by items on the original F scale. Using as subjects 86 males "enrolled in psychology, history and religion courses" and his own semi-structured interview as a measure of "identity status," Marcia found only low or insignificant correlations between identity status and a variety of other variables that should have given it some "construct validity."

Instead of discarding "identity" forthwith, Marcia claims that his own semistructured interview goes far to providing a measure of the "identity statuses" (p. 558). In fact, the only finding worth noting is a significant discrimination in performance on the F scale between those categorized under the labels "identity achievement" and "foreclosure." What this might mean is anybody's guess, partly because the California F scale has been discarded long ago as a psychometric instrument and partly because somebody might "foreclose" on non-authoritarian parents.

It is significant that in the 1970s Erikson began to clarify the meaning of "identity" by relating it to the social context. In *Ghandi's Truth*, he discovered that British imperialism, and by implication American economic imperialism at the time of his writing, could destroy the communal "identity" or culture) of the exploited territory (1969, pp. 265-266, 269-270) and excite racial prejudice in the counterpart (p. 191). In this political and economic context, "ego identity" is more clearly defined as a commitment to the parts of a cultural heritage (economic, political, cultural and spiritual) considered to be important by the individual. For example, the culturally important Indian textile industry, based on manual skills, was destroyed by the British, and textile products were imported from the machine-based industry established in Britain. Again, the educational system replaced Indian culture with the British variety. Certainly, when Erikson (1973) had to debate with Huey Newton in the early 1970s, he was not poorly prepared, although he still believed, in characteristic psychoanalytic (and cognitive) style, that social forces were unleashed by personal conflicts. Thus Vietnam and Watergate are attributed to "the *repression* of inner conflict in those who overadjust to power, the *suppression* of adversary opinions, and the ready *oppression* of foreign people..." (Erikson, 1974, pp. 110-111). This switch of opinion about the "American character" is seen as "political" by Gutmann (p. 64) who believes that Erikson's older view is consistent with such changes in the American scene as a decline in racism and sexism—a point which must be news to Coles (1976), Frady (1980) and Geng (1976)— and the landslide victory in 1972 of Nixon. "Would a nation whose psyche was peopled with sinister fantasies of otherness have so eagerly embraced the architect of the opening to China or of the overtures to the Soviet Union?" (Gutmann, p. 64). The answer to the latter question is "yes." As Yankelovich (1972) has pointed out, support for Nixon came from the fact that he had outfaced both Communist powers which did not postpone his visits to their capitals despite the fact that he had ordered the mining of Haiphong Harbour. This appeal to "jingoism" was successful. Once again a psychologist like Gutmann becomes a naif as he attempts to interpret uncontrolled events beyond the reach of scientific methods.

The early (pre-1968) work of Erikson was a part of the general intellectual culture and common parlance, but not of the scientific study of people during the dominance of the liberal consensus. The reasons are not hard to find. First he was an optimistic developmental theorist, recognizing that man is capable of integrating his aptitudes and social roles to form an identity and "that society, in principle, tends to be so constituted ..." (1963, p. 270) as to encourage the individual to move through all his stages. Second, the notion that man had a unique identity which he achieved after suffering an "identity crisis" was attractive to young social intellectuals who often found themselves at odds with a crass material society in which money controlled man (instead of the reverse) with what they took to be apalling consequences to man and the environment. Erikson made no contribution to that unrealistic hybrid to which he was committed, "psychoanalytic science"; a more accurate judgment, based on some empirical evidence, would place him with Rogers, Maslow and Allport as a writer toying seriously with pleasant ideas that appealed to a large number of educated people. Gergen (1973) lists these ideas as the "heavy value placed on uniqueness or individuality" (p. 314) and, reciprocally, a dislike of being dumped in a conventional clinical category which purports to explain behavior. This makes Erikson neither a psychologist nor a realist until he came to grips with the solid world in his later writings, by which time his services were no longer required because consensus ideas were under attack from a more dangerous quarter. New concepts were required which would focus attention on the "inner man" to the detriment of the social milieu in which that person was embedded.

F. Values Clarification

By the early 1970s it had become very clear to Bruner (1971a) that his former emphasis on codes, structures and the reconstruction of the curriculum had been of little value to the average child during the "disturbing years" (p. ix) of student dissidence and the "ruinous and cruel war in Vietnam" (p. x).

> How could a society . . . wage a war in the name of a generous way of life while our own way of life included urban ghettos, a culture of poverty, racism, etc. We looked afresh at the appalling effects of poverty and racism on the lives of children and the extent to which schools had become instruments of the evil forces in our society (ibid.).

The solution propounded was the emphasis on teaching values at the expense of that on knowledge structures. This is the old vacuous hope, expressed by Dewey (1897, p. 17), that personal improvement in the lives of most people can be brought about within unchanged social institutions. After Watergate, the task became more salient. As Etzioni (1976) remarked: "it is the school's job to educate students morally . . . over and above the prevalent societal standards" (p. 66). Specifically, exercises in values clarification may "help the student gain insight into why he values what he does, and foster greater self-awareness" (p. 45). If, as Etzioni argues, the student learns "moral principles," then the compromises he must reach "later on" with people in an admittedly corrupt society will be less unethical than they would have been without these principles at all.

This line of argument—that "values clarification" will lead to the acceptance of "moral principles" which, in turn, will result in better than average moral behaviour—has weaknesses. (a) As MacIntyre (1958) had pointed out, we can all agree about abstract values (peace, love, freedom, happiness and so on), but we have no way of linking them to our concrete problems (threats of war, urban blight, poverty, inflation) and indeed attempts at this sort of linkage nearly always provoke unproductive dissent. (b) Values have little connection with behavior. For example, Milgram (1974) demonstrated in a summary of his 1960s researches into obedience to authority, that most of his subjects, who were delivering apparently severe electric shocks during an experimental enquiry supposedly into the learning of word pairs, reported previously that they were peace loving and non-aggressive. As Milgram concludes, "The force exerted by the moral sense of the individual is less effective than social myth would have us believe. . . . Moral factors can be shunted aside with relative ease by calculated restructuring of the informational and social field" (pp. 6-7). (c) Again, Etzioni assumes that the teachers have some countervailing power against an admittedly corrupt society. Since he has no evidence that teachers can perform that function—indeed, ever could in all of their history as a professional group—then opposite opinions can be aired. "There is no alchemy by which education can turn into fine gold the base metal of a distracted and materially-minded age" (in Robertson, 1969, p. 222). Even Etzioni has to agree that "most schools cannot proceed very far in promoting values not shared by the community at large" (p. 66). Since the only communities where people come together because they have common aims, aspirations, values and so on, are the family and friendship, it would seem that the school has no scope for performing its values calrification function effectively (Varenne, 1978, p. 74). Teachers who accept the burden of this function will be the target of its criticism when the depressed post-Keynesian American economy unearths a disproportionately large amount of adult criminals and sullen adolescents.

In the face of these problems, a usable theory of moral development has to play down the influence of the milieu which was explicit in Hartshorne and May (1928-29) who discovered, using objective tests, that the level of a youngster's honesty was specific to domains and settings in which group approval and example played a part. Kohlberg (1972) does not quarrel with the psychometric quality of Hartshorne and May's investigation but with what he considers to be their "nihilism" (1972, p. 196). That is, he believes that his own interpretation of their findings, "carried to its logical conclusion," suggests that "concepts of good or bad conduct were psychologically irrelevant and that moral conduct, like other conduct, could be expressed "in terms of the child's needs, his group values, and the demands of the situation" (ibid.). This position upsets Kohlberg who believes that it sanctions cheating if the outcomes are consistent with "the great American standard of success" (p. 196).

In this unpleasant situation, reinforced by what Kohlberg and Gilligan (1972) see as the questioning of all forms of social order by youth in the 1960s (p. 147), the new theory had to assume that the potential for moral awareness and its development via cognitive transformations characterized the individual as a human being. Fortunately Kohlberg (1971) had acceptable precedents for using this theoretical tactic: "Following Dewey and Piaget I shall argue that the goal of moral education is the stimulation of "natural" development of the individual's own moral development capacities, thus allowing him to use his own moral judgement to control behavior" (p. 71). Tucked away in this theory is the idealistic notion of human universals. For example, in dealing with the learning of sex-roles, Kohlberg (1966) argues that "observational learning" emphasized by social learning theorists "is cognitive in the sense that it is selective and internally organized by relational schemata rather than directly reflecting associaton of events in the outside world" (p. 53). These schemata, as he had previously remarked in a 1963 paper, "represent structures emerging from the interaction with his social environment, rather than directly reflecting external structures given by the child's culture" (p. 30). This is a highly cognitive, idealistic position.

Theoretically, this fitted neatly into the programme of the liberal consensus, as did the sequence of stages of moral development emanating from it which ran from behaviour dictated by selfish concerns (Stage 1 and 2) to that directed by moral principles (Stages 5 and 5). An early awkward finding was that most subjects tested fall into Stages 3 and 4 in which the individual conforms to avoid disapproval and censure by others, particularly legitimate authorities. Disappointing too was the fact that Stages 5 and 6 were comparatively empty of subjects, especially in non-industrialized societies, although presumably this maldistribution might be altered by appropriate moral education. There is no evidence that this is the case. Indeed, these societies, underdeveloped or forcibly developed because of the low wages paid for menial labour (South Korea, Taiwan), are usually presided over by dictators who have no interest in supporting the teaching of moral principles.

Apart from the telling work of Milgram (1974) and Zimbardo (1973) on adult obedience to authority, the main flaw in Kohlberg's researches lies in the psychometric weakness of his Moral Judgement Scale consisting of nine dilemmas which he administered to 72 "middle-class" and "lower-class" boys, ages 10, 13 and 16 years, in Chicago. From the protocols he derived his six developmental stages of moral reasoning. Kurtines and Greif (1975) point out this was the main finding from Kohlberg's 1958 doctoral thesis (p. 454). There is no point in describing in detail the convincing atttack on the Scale launched by Kurtines and Greif: that it has never been published and the scoring system is so awkward that only someone trained by Kohlberg is regarded as accurate enough to do the job—a practice in marked opposition to that in the physical and biological science; that the probing questions asked by the interviewer and the number of dilemmas used vary across studies so that the results from different investigations are quite unstable (p. 455); since the characters in the dilemmas are all males, it is not surprising that females perform at a morally less mature level than males (p. 456); no conventional measures of the reliability of the Scale have been reported (pp. 456-458) and the predictive validities are not compelling, being readily accounted for by other variables (p. 460); there is no consistent evidence that the sequence of stages is invariant (pp. 461-466) and the ordering of the two top (most principled) stages has been questioned in an empirical study (p. 467), and there is no cross-cultural support for the idealistic idea of a universality of stages (pp. 461-462). Indeed, the evidence is clear that moral judgments are influenced by the behaviour of various models and, because of that, exhibit inconsistencies and disparities over time (Bandura, 1969, p. 278). There may be stages in moral development but not of Kohlberg's sort in which they are said to appear regardless of the child's exposure to adult remarks about what is good and bad, and to adult behaviour (Phillips and Kelly, p. 372).

A final point should be made: Stage 6, "Morality of individual principles based on conscience" and Stage 5, "Morality of contract and of democratically accepted law," represent the responses of a small percentage of samples in industrialized representative democracies, and of no one in primitive societies. For example in a study reported by Sullivan (1977, p. 41), about 85 percent of adolescents were at Stage 4 or less, and the modal group characterizing more than 60 percent of the sample was at Stage 3 (trying to earn approval by helping or pleasing other people). This would seem to render too formal one of Sullivan's criticisms of Kohlberg: that his system of moral development reflects the "liberal ideology" which rose in Britain (John Locke, Adam Smith) and France (the thinkers of the Enlightenment) to sanction a rising capitalism and the scientific and technological advances that supported it (p. 3). The legalistic and formalistic categories of such an ideology are unlikely to appeal to many.

What most people have learned is that, in a society which combines human civil rights (if they can be paid for) with the exploitation of ordinary people (who usually can't pay for them), it is essential for survival to get along with other people, to make useful contacts, and to avoid being iconoclastic, however justified this attitude may be. These are the most valuable social arrangements they learn. Sullivan's refusal to accept this possibility, replacing it with an attack on "liberal ideology," is reflected in his support of "a caring society" (p. 34) which has some vague connection with unspecified religious feelings: "The creation, development, and substance of the human community is at its very core a deeply personal and therefore ultimately religious event" (p. 35).

There are two problems here. (a) "A deeply-personal event" need not necessarily be "a religious event" and both concepts are the unlikely basis of a contemporary "human community" like the suburbs or the slums. In particular, "the human society" and "religious" represent an emotional *cri du coeur* rather than any concepts ever realized in human history. Religion has been associated with authoritarian dogmas and violence for a long time (Koestler, 1967, p. 234). (b) A "caring society" is unlikely to come about because of a "radical cultural change": the latter can only be a consequence of radical economic changes which are nowhere on the horizon. Indeed in the contemporary economic depression into which the Western industrialized world has sunk, a non-caring society of *sauve qui peut* is more probable (Friedenberg, 1976), in which case Etzioni's observation— "most schools cannot proceed very far in promoting values not shared by the community at large" (1976, p. 66)—spells the doom of Kohlberg. In fact, books on human development, which routinely used to have a chapter on "values" by Kohlberg, now sport authors dealing with "maturity" and "socialization" (Hetherington and Parke, 1977).

Of course, there has been a great deal of work, inspired by Bandura rather than Kohlberg, dealing with children's cooperation and helping (Bryan, 1975), cooperative behaviour (Cook and Stingle, 1974), altruism (Bryan and London, 1970) and prosocial behaviour (Staub, 1975). All attest to a new concern with the positive aspects of moral behaviour in children, but none pays attention to the countervailing, negative features of modern life (the media, columns about trivia, white-collar crime, looting, terrorists, guerillas, widespread corruption) which are likely, at best, to extinguish these positive behaviours and, at worst, to replace them with their immoral counterparts. *Pari passu*, on the industrial front, jobs formerly demanding highly-paid skills are being so completely automated that workers have become depressed and trust no one in authority (Lasch, 1979, p. 309). Unlike Lasch, however, who is aware of the dubious practice of dealing with people apart from their social milieu, some psychologists try to look on the bright side.

G. Trust

In a liberal society in which groups are played against one another for the maintenance of social order (Karabel 1979), lying is endemic. This was more obviously the case in the middle of the 1960s when American military policies were less successful than advertised and financial affairs were more than usually mismanaged (in 1966 a necessary increase in taxes to pay for the Vietnam War was not exacted). Rotter (1967) chose that time to introduce a self-report measurement of "interpersonal trust," defined as an expectation, generalized from one significant social agent to another, that promises will be kept (Rotter, 1967, p. 653). Believing that trust is desirable for the survival of a group, for a "healthy personality" (p. 651), he provides a few sample items of his Interpersonal Trust Scale (ITS), reports its low test-retest reliabilities (pp. 655-666) and miniscule correlations with other variables which might be regarded as likely correlates (p. 662). In other words, the ITS is neither reliable nor valid. In 1980, after some socially and financially dismal years for the United States, Rotter (1980) returns to his theme, still using the ITS. Without describing the curve of distribution of his subjects (most are university students if only because an understanding of the items would be beyond average people), and the percentage of subjects in the "low" and "high" category of "trusters," he believes that the former group are under no "moral pressure" (p. 3) to do anything but lie and cheat because "everybody else is doing it to them." By contrast, the latter group "acts morally" (p. 4).

Rotter is honest enough to admit that he can find no stable relationship between performance on the ITS and estimates of the critical variable "gullability" (p. 6) and that he has never tested (one wonders why) the poorer sorts of people who, subject to all the pressures of an inequitable society, are more likely to be "low trusters" and yet represent the largest group in society. Why, it must be surmised, did Rotter bother to study such a dimension, vacuous in the social sense and psychometrically unserviceable? It is worthwhile postponing the answer until another variable, "altruism," is discussed.

H. Altruism

Kanfer (1979) believes in the commonly-held erroneous idea of a brilliant American past now come to dust. "The combination of social and personal controls that has existed for two centuries in the United States seems to have been adequate to maintain a strong and cohesive society" (Kanfer, 1979, p. 234). He forgets the unpleasant conflicts in the late nineteenth century stemming from battles between management and labour (Hobsbawm, 1975), the illegal military and paramilitary ways of putting down dissidence (Alexander, 1976), the divisive activity of the House Committee on Un-American Activities (Goodman, 1969) and of Senator McCarthy. His "social cohesiveness" appears to refer to the fact that, at least until the 1960s and early 1970s, violence was never unleashed against the state (Hofstadter, 1971, p. 11). Indeed most of Kanfer's indicators of change for the worse have always characterised America as an industrial society; at best the "change" simply indicates an increase in their amount. Take, for example, "an increased frequency and severity of social destruction" (Kanfer, p. 234), largely a euphemism for race riots. These existed before 1960 for an obvious reason, increased during the 1960s and 1970s but now appear to have decreased although the 1980 Miami riot and the recession may spark another round of social action by irritated people who have the most to lose in a depressed economy.

Kanfer plans to stop this destruction of a "cohesive society" in a psychological way by linking experimentally-based self-generated control to the altruistic concern for others (p. 235). Specifically, the less-rewarding low-probability altruistic behaviour must become the most preferred behaviour which brings personal and social rewards (p. 236). This can be brought about, according to Kanfer, by "a teacher or a therapist" (p. 237) praising the person for self-initiated altruistic behaviour. While Kanfer offers some examples of "reciprocal helping" and "family therapy" in "cooperative projects," he says nothing about the smallness and ineffectiveness of such an approach in the larger society which is responsible for the egocentricity in the first place. A "liberal society," in Macpherson's (1965) sense, promotes "possesive individualism" and the United States was originally and still is the most liberal of all societies. This point was noticed in 1844 by Marx.

> None of the supposed rights of man . . . go beyond the egoistic man, man as he is, as a member of society; that is, an individual separated from the community, withdrawn into himself, wholly preoccupied with his private interest and acting in accordance with his private caprice. Man is far from being considered, in the rights of man, as a species-being; on the contrary, species-life itself—society— appears as a system which is external to the individual and as a limitation of his original independence. The only bond between men is natural necessity, need and private interest, the preservation of their property and egoistic persons (in Bottomore, 1964, p. 26).

So much for Kanfer.

Why, then, spend time on "altruism" and "trust"? A clear answer is that there is no tolerable alternative except those that are more dismal. America is in a time of recession with leaders and advisers of poor quality, a banking system balanced precariously, its currency of dubious value, parts of its manufacturing capacity declining rapidly, and its sources of cheap energy dissipated. Only psychologists have enough gall to ignore these facts of life in a decaying economic empire because they play with speculations and malleable data. They are the perfect bringers of good news in the bad times of a society badly in need of secular redemption.

It must be concluded that these concepts are no more useful and scientific than the larger theories from which they are drawn. Worse, despite disclaimers, many of the concepts are in harmony with the established social order. This happens partly because they attract funds, but a more important reason is that the criterion for their acceptability is not their scientific status or usefulness but their attractiveness, a point made by Gergen (1973). They are part of the "mission-oriented research" bringing the necessary dreams when the social edifice is crumbling. They tell what comfortable people would like to hear, and, despite what Hodgson (1976, pp. 479-484) has to say about the errors social intellectuals make when dealing with class concepts, most psychologists speak to comfortable "middle class" people. For example, Zimbardo (1980) has recently mentioned the terrible problem of "isolation" and "indifference" in contemporary American society, contrasting these with the way "immigrants, blacks, minority groups" *in the past* (italics mine) have "maintained their dignity by reaffirming family values and by tightening the bonds of friendship" (Zimbardo, 1980, p. 76). It is pleasant (and necessary) to believe that human problems are psychological and modifiable when their source is the unchangeable nature of the social order.

5 / THE MESSIANIC TRADITION IN EDUCATION DECLINES

Prominent American educators had always believed that "education alone could bring into being a more ideal social order or raise the individual to a higher level of moral existence . . ." (Bowers, 1969, p. 203). Even as late as 1970 Schrag contended that "the school is the answer to Karl Marx—and to everything else" although "the school system has failed" (Schrag, 1970, p. 68). To this end the help of a psychological science had been considered essential even before Thorndike put his personal stamp on the idea (Joncich, 1968, p. 166) and had been revived during the 1950s and 1960s when it was widely assumed that psychologists should be involved in the demonstration that academic programmes for preschoolers had some benefits. For example, Hunt (1961), a psychologist without any experience of teaching, amassed a great deal of information purporting to show that "intelligence" or "intellectual capacity," the supposed requirement for performance in symbolic skills, was not genetically determined or static but malleable and plastic and that, therefore, the cognitive performance of disadvantaged children could be improved, regardless of the quality of the milieu. And so in the summer of 1965, a Head Start programme was introduced to improve the achievement of underprivileged children and, in the long run, to reduce poverty; indeed it was a quickly-implemented part of the war on poverty undertaken by the Johnson Administration in 1964 (Smith and Bissell, 1970, p. 56). People knowledgeable about the troubled state of cognitive psychology as a science and the existence of many ad hoc programmes, locally controlled, launched in an ad hoc way and taught by teachers with no special preparation, would not have expected such an educational enterprise to counteract the powerful anti-educational influence of a slum environment. Despite its associated benefits of social work and preventive medicine, it could not provide "the promise of America" (Pines, 1967, p. 11) in the sense of promoting social mobility. Support for such scepticism came about the time the liberal consensus was falling apart in the late 1960s. As Hodgson (1980) points out, that consensus was a mixture of national (liberal) and international (conservative) policies appealing to as many voters as possible, and it was

> firmly based on the belief in infinitely receding new frontiers of economic growth. Out of the cornucopia of wealth that would be won from growth, social needs could be met and social tensions—including racial tensions—could be resolved without the conflict between competing classes that was the basis of the old politics (Hodgson, 1980, p. 243).

By 1968 it had become obvious that the blacks had not been appeased in their search for better status, that economic growth could not exist without inflation and that Communism abroad had not been contained without a socially divisive war. It was the fate of some authors to show that liberal reform was not possible by educational changes.

A. Coleman, Jensen and Jencks

Coleman (1966) was the first to supply data showing that the school was ineffective in creating equal educational opportunity. He found a marked educational discrepancy between minority and white schools and that this increased with age, but that the variation in achievement was largely associated with parental commitment to education. When this variable was partialled out, factors "such as the amount of money spent per pupil, or the number of books in the library, or physical facilities such as gymnasiums or cafeterias or laboratories, seemed to make no appreciable difference to the child's level of achievement" (Hodgson, 1976, p. 448).

This was the signal for a display of statistical argument about the appropriateness of the analysis employed by Coleman, about his interpretation of the data, and even about the value of the data from schools in a society which discriminated against minority groups (Cohen and Garet, 1975, pp. 32-33). Bowles and Gintis (1976, p. 8) argue that only "far-reaching social changes" can produce "schools which promote economic equality and positive human development," ignoring the fact that the Russians also have not been strikingly successful in this matter (Szamuely, 1970, p. 53). About the only conclusion that can be drawn from this squabbling, and from the one about to be described, is that research with human beings cannot deliver promised results on a topic laced with value judgments and that, therefore, the American plan to change society by improving people in schools never had a chance of being successful. The Coleman Report, with its attendant verbal fights, was the first attack on the ideas of the liberal consensus. In a short letter, Coleman (1972) returned to his theme that busing and compensatory education would have only a marginal improvement on the educational achievement of poor children (black and white), that equal educational opportunity could not be provided by the State but only by the loving care and attention of parents, and that any integration should exist not because of an increase in educational attainment it might bring, but because blacks and whites should get to know each other. These ideas added fuel to the segregation controversy.

The next blows came in 1969. In April, the Westinghouse Ohio National Evaluation of Head Start showed that even full year programmes produced only marginal gains that did not persist into the elementary grades (Cicirelli, Evans and Schiller, 1970, pp. 123-124). As Jensen (1969) has phrased the matter, "The chief goal of compensatory education... has been utterly unrealized in any of the large compensatory programmes that have been evaluated so far" (p. 3). And then he went on to resurrect one deadly explanation for this state of affairs: he argued that the Head Start enterprise could never succeed anyway because intelligence, the driving force behind educational performance, was largely inherited and not to be improved or boosted by any kind of educational intervention. The ensuing uproar among intellectuals over Jensen's paper has already been described and need not detain us here (Jensen, 1972). The hereditarian conception of intelligence always had racial overtones since its assimilation by certain American psychologists, a point noted first by Karier in 1972, and it had reappeared in a 1966 book on general psychology written by H.E. Garrett, a student of Thorndike (Karier, 1976, p. 132). Kamin's 1974 account elaborated Karier's point by referring to professional writing of the 1920s and 1930s (Kamin, 1977, p. 31) and he simply assumed that the modern exponents of the hereditarian position like Jensen were racists too, unjustifiably discriminating against American blacks. Moreover, this position appeared to transgress the popular American notion of progress (Heilbroner, 1960) and, worst of all for the supporters of the liberal consensus, its most trenchant critic was a behaviorist in the Watsonian tradition who believed that intellectual improvement required concurrent social changes which he did not specify (Kamin, p. 229). The angry struggle between those who stressed the relatively strong hereditarian impact on intelligence (Jensen, 1978; Gourlay, 1978) and those who favoured the view that the environment was the formative influence is another example of the conceptual squabbling that goes far to supporting Medawar's (1977) contention that psychology is a non-science which cannot resolve controversial issues.

Equally unpalatable to the liberal consensus was the work of Jencks and his associates (1972) who showed that the school had no effect on economic inequality, the spread of income in which "the best-paid fifth of all white workers earn 600% more than the worst-paid fifth" and white workers earned 50% more than their black counterparts. From his finding that, despite school reform over the last 30 years, the uneven distribution of income has remained static, Jencks concludes that "As long as egalitarians assume that public policy cannot contribute to economic equality directly, but must proceed by ingenious manipulation of marginal institutions like the schools, progress will remain glacial" (p. 265). The final inference runs:

If we want to move beyond this tradition (of relying on the schools for producing social change), we will have to establish political control over the economic institutions that run our society. That is what other countries usually call socialism. Anything less will end in the same disappointment as the reforms of the 1960s (ibid.).

Oddly enough, the findings of Jencks and his associates have been supported by a quasi-experimental study by Firkowska and her associates (1978) in Warsaw. Because this city had been largely razed during the Second World War, political authorities had it rebuilt so that there was an even distribution throughout the city of families from every social class. Despite this strategy of destroying the usual association between social class (education and occupation) and quality of the milieu, Firkowska found, in the case of the 1974 performances on Raven's Matrices and two attainment tests by children born in 1963, correlations among these variables that were as high as those reported by Jencks for American children. Speaking of this association between social class and "mental performance," Firkowska comments: "Despite this social policy of equalization, the association persists in a form characteristic of more traditional societies" (Firkowska et al., p. 1362). It goes without saying, however, that the Polish study militates against Jenck's support for large-scale social reforms as a cure for inequalities: as Firkowska remarks, "social changes over a generation have failed to override forces that determine the social class distributions of mental performance among children" (ibid). As with Coleman, these "forces," according to the Polish authors, lie in the upbringing of the children of occupationally superior parents who place great stress on good performance in school, although an equally plausible inference is that these parents were genetically superior.

B. Attacking Jensen

Contemporary American social intellectuals dislike studies supporting the largely hereditarian basis of symbolic performances that discriminate between privileged and underprivileged groups and they used at least five strategies for counterattacking Jensen. The first was an exhortation to better teaching (Kamin); the second emphasized mastery of a chunk of information before procession to the next chunk (Bloom); the third was teaching the cognitive processes underlying the IQ tests (Estes, Sternberg); the fourth was a change in the items so that minority groups would not be in such a disadvantaged position (Fallows); and the fifth was to stay with Head Start, reliance being placed on new, and possibly more hopeful, studies (Zigler, Darlington, et. al.). These strategies will be discussed in turn.

Kamin's (1977) 1974 attack on Burt and Jensen's conception of the heritability of IQ test scores has substance since Burt's data on which it is based is certainly fraudulent (Hearnshaw, 1979), although Eysenck (1979) has reported that his own researches support Burt's position. What is peculiar about Kamin is his lack of any political sense, evident in his assertion that "the promises of behaviorism applied to human affairs cannot be realized without social and political reform" (Kamin, 1979, p. 229). Since the economic situation of American blacks has worsened in the last twenty years (Frady, 1980, p. 15), Kamin's stance is futile. This is true also of Gould (1980) who argues that the significant difference in average IQ between American blacks and whites is to be attributed to different social conditions. The California solution has been to ban the use of standardized tests on which minority groups perform poorly, thus effectively preventing any further investigations, the emergence of fresh findings about the social basis of any unjustifiable discrimination (Opton, 1979) and the eradication of tests which set a desirable standard of academic performance. Kamin (1980) goes the length of arguing that even if IQ tests *were* shown to be "racially neutral, unbiassed predictors of school performance" (p. 120), he would still not allow them to be used for placing children in EMR classes because the goal is equal educational opportunity for all and the business of teachers is not to give tests but to teach so well that no children will need to be placed in these classes. Unfortunately, the selection of teachers and their current performance makes this an unrealistic position (*Time*, June 16, 1980), as does historical information (Collins, 1979, p. 18).

Second, Bloom (1979) believes that his Mastery Learning Programme can help anyone achieve "common levels of attainment" although, as he admits, "after different lengths of instructional time." The instructional system is divided into three very familiar parts. First, the instructional objectives are to be defined (task analysis). Second, the instructional programme is to be divided into instructional units, each of which has a teaching, testing and remedial phase until the unit has been mastered and the pupil can advance to the next unit. Third, instruction after failure is designed to eradicate mistakes and inculcate new knowledge necessary to understand the unit in question and wrongly assumed to be in the youngster's possession. Bloom argues that the initial negative correlation between IQ and time taken to master a unit became much smaller with the increase in the number of units taken.

This presents three problems. First, in financially stringent times, some attention must be paid to the cost-benefit problem, especially in the case of the large number of sub-average students who might take up a great deal of time to reach criterion level. Second, Bloom presumes that the instruction is teacher-proof, that teachers with a wide range of competence could achieve the same results, a most unlikely event. Third, there is the administrative problem: what happens to the more competent students while their less fortunate counterparts are being brought up to scratch?

Estes (1974) was worried about "the changing mood of society " (1974, p. 749) in the direction of resisting the administration of intelligence tests for predictive purposes. His strategy was to make the tests diagnostic by interpreting the processes underlying test behaviour and by localizing and improving the deficits in performance revealed by test scores. The vocabulary test, in which the individual is asked to define or explain a word, is subdivided into daunting "processes." Accurate performance on this test depends on "specific retrieval strategies" and "the availability of retrieval cues, an individual who is asked to give the meaning of a word may do so at various levels from associates of the word, and differentiate it from others in cues, an individual who is asked to give the meaning of a word may do so at various levels from associates of the word and differentiate it from others in the long-term memory system (p. 746). Then Estes adds a caveat with social implications he avoids considering. This refers to the fact that the acceptability of a child's answer will be very much determined by living in a home "with numerous opportunities and occasions to inquire concerning the meanings of words and to have these explained to him by parents and siblings..." (ibid.). The problem here is that, since 60 per cent of the U.S. population is working class in the sense that they derive their incomes by manual labour (Hodgson, 1976, p. 481), the "average home," especially in the current economic recession, is not sufficiently cultivated or sophisticated to provide the sort of corrective verbal feedback envisaged by Estes. The presence of the ubiquitous TV set may not help matters.

Further problems appear in his account of the processes underlying performance in a vocabulary test. Success may be attributable to a "combination of inherent capacities and past experiences" (p. 746). But failure is attributed to many different sources.

> Inability to explain or define a word on request may occur because the necessary memory structure has never been established, because of a lack of retrieval cues for an intact memory structure, because words required to express the definition are at a low availability owing to disuse, or because the individual lacks a general conception of the required solution to the type of problem and thus gives an answer which is meaningful within his own frame of reference but not within that of the examiner (pp. 746-747).

This approach by Estes suffers from at least four problems. (a) Logically, if a good performance in sorts of items is due in part, to "inherent capacities," failure must equally by due, in part, to a relative absence of these capacities, a point understandably ignored by Estes. (b) If performance on the item can be improved by training, the appropriate question is for how long that training can sustain that effect? The effect of practice on the items themselves certainly lasts for only a short period of time (Jensen, 1972, p. 183). (c) Training students to acquire the necessary memory structure, retrieval cues and so on would require an enormous expenditure of funds which depressed economies are unlikely to provide, especially in the light of deteriorating student performance over the years (Armbruster, 1977). (d) Attempts to provide illiterate minority groups with elementary training at the university level have been unsuccessul (Gross, 1978).

The only function of Estes' programmes was to reduce the inflammation in the nature-nurture controversy, which had reappeared viciously in the early 1970s, by encouraging researchers to train youngsters in the sub-skills which apparently underlay the putatively-inherited abilities that had fallen into disrepute at that time. Estes' own suggestion that his programme "might lead to long-term social gains" (p. 749) is an unrealistic hope (IQ and educational performance can be improved by coaching) which does not merit serious discussion because, in the best of circumstances, the debilitating effects of a slum environment and of parents uninterested in the educational process will provide a barrier that mere coaching cannot surmount.

Layzer (1972) once stated less stridently than Watson a famous behaviouristic position: "I know of no theoretical or experimental evidence to contradict the assumption that everyone in the normal range of intelligence could, if sufficiently motivated, and given sufficient time, acquire the basic cognitive abilities demanded by such professions as law, medicine, and business administration" (Layzer, 1972, p. 296). Even if Layzer's position is accepted that IQ performance is largely determined by environmental variables, especially a slum milieu and correlated poor teaching by understandably unenthusiastic teachers, the problem becomes one of finding a change agent since the authorities intend to do nothing either about the slums or about the quality of the teachers. This problem was made worse by the discovery of a significant decline in the average score on the Scholastic Aptitude Test (SAT) which was widely used as a partial screening mechanism for entry into universities (Tavris, 1976). The explanation offered by Tavris for this decrease in intelligence did not rely on "race, genetics, income, or social class" (Tavris, 1976, p. 69). Borrowed from Zajonc (1976), it was an inference that from 1962 until 1974, the baby boom babies were growing to adolescence and that they were so large in number per family and so close together in age as to prevent the parents having enough time to pay enough attention to them, especially to their performance in school (p. 71). Tavris predicted that the reduction in births in the 1960s and their being more spaced out in age would arrest the slump in IQ so that signs of an increase in SAT scores would show themselves by 1980.

This explanation is invaluable because it implicates neither the society nor teaching nor hereditary factors, although 78 other explanations have been advanced (Zajonc and Bargh, 1980, p. 662). Unfortunately, birth order and SAT connection can be falsified, and Zajonc and Bargh have reported in a careful study that "if nothing but birth order had contributed to the (downward average 1970-1977 SAT) trend we should have observed a decline of 2.6 points instead of 30.1 points" (p. 664). However, despite this, Zajonc and Bargh are unwilling to let go of the small birth-order effect. It may be "weak," they argue (p. 668), but could be seen to better advantage in larger groups; in any case, it may be the only one to covary systematically with SAT scores.

Sternberg's (1977; 1978a; 1978b; 1979a, 1979b) solution is more convoluted and sly. In a popular article (1979a) he argued that the test constructors had deliberately made "intelligence" into a mystery because they did not know what they were measuring and that this was so because the tests were not based on any "viable theories" (Sternberg, 1979a, p. 42). Although this idea is palpably false, nevertheless it allows Sternberg to introduce to a lay audience an old idea—that intelligence could be described in terms of information processing—as if it were his own creation. "For the first time," he announces, "we have a theory of how that process (solving test items by successful information processing) works" (Sternberg, ibid.). It is a large claim, but it allows him (1978b, p. 117) to dodge the average decline in SAT scores by asking which of the informative processes underlying the IQ items (problem-types) had declined, the implication being that he could repair this deficiency in the hierarchy of information-processing components into which each problem-type could be decomposed.

It is interesting that Sternberg's approach to the tasks and their decomposition into processes is very formal and logical. For example, he divides them into inductive tasks (analogies and metaphorical completions, classification and series-completion problems) and deductive tasks (linear syllogisms and categorical syllogisms) and then, again without finding out how children try to solve the tasks, simply proposes *himself* the "component processes . . . sufficient to solve all problems of this kind (analogies" (Sternberg, 1978a, p. 280). Sternberg's very logical processes differ slightly from task to task (and each account of any one task is rarely the same among his presentations), an example being the processes with the label IMAJER (inference, mapping, application, justification, encoding, and response), which are responsible ("sufficient" in Sternberg's slippery psychological-logical term) for solving an analogy task. For example, take the analogy *lawyer* is to *client* as *doctor* is to *(a) medicine, (b) patient*. Encoding would then refer to the attributes and their values of the initial term; inference is the discovery of the relationship between *lawyer* and *client*; mapping is the establishment of the relationship between first and third terms (*lawyers* and *doctors* are *professionals*: the subject *then* applies *doctor* to each of the two possibilities and justifies the option preferred and the response, presumably *patient*, is given (Sternberg, 1979b, p. 225).

All this is much more complicated than Spearman's (1923) eduction of relations (finding the relationship) and the eduction of correlates (extrapolating from the relationship and the given third term to find the answer, the correlate). Sternberg (1979b, p. 215) takes this point but argues that there are advantages to translating the larger eductions into his finer information-processing concepts (subtasks). The most important of these alleged "advantages" is that the finer concepts are "content-free" and "can be valuable when one wants to test alternative predictions about global stages of information processing" (p. 220). Another advantage is that the information-processing components would not be confounded (this said confounding of items was considered important by Binet) and a diagnosis of the task performance would be available (p. 221).

Since these are arguments, the possibility should be considered that Spearman's relational concepts are just as useful for Sternberg's purposes—and as free of content (Isaacs, 1970). This possibility is not considered, let alone tested, presumably because Spearman is an "old theorist." Moreover, the variety of items in an IQ test (verbal, non-verbal and achievement tasks) has always been regarded as useful, and Sternberg has never demonstrated that he can diagnose weaknesses any better than a conventional intelligence tester.

The empirical results from Sternberg's information-processing finer analysis are unimpressive in contrast to the grand claims of the "new" theory. In an early study (Sternberg, 1977) of analogical reasoning, analogies were divided into the only four possible "precues" or prompts for helping the subject to get the right answers to a two-term analogical problem with the final correlate omitted (A is to B as C is to D1, D2?). The four precues were zero information, which would not allow the generation of any attributes; A (one term) like *lawyer*, probably giving off a variety of random and subjective attributes; A:B (two term, *lawyer:client*), which would certainly begin to reduce the number of feasible relations) and A:B:C (three term, *lawyer:client:doctor*) when the correct correlate should begin to appear. Sometimes Sternberg offers four-terms (with the wrong answer) and five terms (with a right and wrong answer) (Sternberg, 1979b, p. 217, pp. 271-272), but these he considers to be "degenerate conditions" in which "the precuing supplies either no information or full information" (p. 220). Nevertheless, for teaching ("presentation trials"), the "degenerate conditions" make up the second part whereas the other "precues" make up the first part. The dependent variable is labelled "response time scores," although in other places he uses the term "solution latencies" (Sternberg, 1977b, p. 211). He professes to be amazed that the correlation between response-time scores and a standard reasoning task decreased with the amount of information given.

Sternberg believes that this is a "counter-intuitive finding," requiring more analysis, which would never have emerged if he had not adopted an information-processing approach to intelligence. On the other hand, the finding can easily be explained in a commonplace way: the provision of more information will reduce the variance of performance on the dependent variable and hence also the correlations with the reasoning test.

He (1979b) also discusses a "metacomponential" analysis of tasks which is a very general way of knowing how to arrange salient strategies for the effective combination of the components in the solution of the problem. A substitute for the homuncular "control over cognitive processes" (p. 226), it is regarded as a source of explanation for the longer time better reasoners spend on encoding the terms of an analogy than do poorer reasoners; the former group do this to generate more attributes for comparison which can be quickly narrowed down to the correct solution in the mapping and application stages (p. 227). Moreover, the fact that older children make fewer "errors" in analogies "can probably be traced at least in part to a decision at the metacomponential level to process information more nearly exhaustively" (ibid.). It might also probably be due to a decline in the number of impulsive people who make choices quickly and commit many errors (McLauchlan, 1977, p. 25).

Why would someone as flashy and muddled as Sternberg gain the limelight in the late 1970s? He has no data worth bothering about; the number of students tested is always small and from the more affluent sections of the community (children of Yale professors, for example), and there has been no attempt to demonstrate that slum children can be taught to learn and retain the processing so that they can make better scores on the tasks and on the intelligence tests of which they make up only a part.

Sternberg's fame rests on this promise, given but never implemented, that psychologists can help school performance in some way. For example, he talks of the "pedagogic value" of his theory, i.e., using it he can pinpoint particular weaknesses which are a source of failure in "global information processing," and can develop strategies for improving performing on global tasks by treating these weaknesses (Sternberg, 1979b, p. 225). He has not accomplished this, although the strategies he proposes (linguistic and spatial) are remarkably similar to Vernon's (1970) V:Ed factor, the rough equivalent of Spearman's "g." Sternberg's career, so far, has illustrated the fact that American psychologists, in a difficult situation, are willing to clutch at any straw, however fragile, to give them a passing show of theoretical stature and usefulness. After all, they are part of a "redeemer society" which badly needs redemption in the standard way. Sternberg to the rescue? Why not? Any port in a storm.

A fourth conceptual attempt to deal with Jensen was made by Fallows (1980) who, unlike Kamin, believed that changing test items to benefit minority groups was the proper procedure for reducing the strong linear relationship between students' scores on the Scholastic Aptitude Test (SAT) and mean family income (Fallows, 1980, p. 34; Educational Testing Service, 1980, pp. 7-8). He ignores the inference that the wealthier attend superior schools whereas slum children had no such advantage, preferring instead the more conceptually awkward, but popular, explanation in terms of unjustifiable racial discrimination and denial of potential. He quotes the opinion of a representative of the National Association of Coloured People (NAACP). "Standardized tests are used from the cradle to the grave to select, reject, stratify, classify, and sort people, and they are used in ways that keep certain segments of the population from realizing their aspirations. Most of all they limit the access of blacks and other minorities to higher education" (p. 38). Fallows accepts this view that people have "reasoning skills" (p. 48) of some sort which might be measured rather than those more appropriate to the professional middle class culture (p. 43). The conclusion is that tests like SAT and GRE (Graduate Record Examination) are unfair; "... far from serving as agents of diversity and social mobility, such tests reinforce and legitimize every inequality that now exists" (p. 39).

Fallows has two other minor grumbles that can be dismissed easily. First, coaching students in what he believes to be not knowledge but "only mastery of an unusual and specialized system of thought" (p. 45) may be effective. If this is the case, why are teachers in slum schools so unwilling to do it? Again why would eminent schools, especially their prestigious applied faculties of law and medicine, want to acquire people with such an "unusual and specialized system of thought?" Second, failing a test according to Fallows (p. 38, p. 84) has a negative effect on a person's self-esteem. However, this is true only if passing a test is regarded as important by that person. Again, many other experiences are unpleasant such as being poor, black and living in a slum. The fact is that attacking tests is a great deal easier than getting rid of the slums and their broken-down schools and apathetic teachers, all of which are a more likely source of poor performance.

Accordingly, since Fallows is stuck with the American plan of social change via conceptual change, obvious in his understanding of "social mobility" as meaning *upward* mobility, he supports the use of tests with a minority bias like "black vocabulary" (p. 46-47). In doing so, he ignores, as others would not, the possibility of reverse discrimination and the fact that aptitude tests are likely to pick out poor children with talent in symbolic skills. Indeed, he meets such a person who is reported as saying: "I believe that standardized tests have benefited American education, and have benefited all the classes, as a very important part of the American meritocratic philosophy" (p. 43). But—and this is the second part of Fallows' affirmative action by way of tests—he simply wants more room at the top of the hierarchy, so much more that, in effect, there would not be much of a hierarchy at all. The means to such an unrealistic goal (Michels, 1915) is the introduction of minority-based test items to "broaden the pool of talent open to colleges" (p. 46), to "expand the pool of talent in more than a hit-or-miss way" (p. 48).

But it is far from a "hit-or-miss way." Universities have discovered that the tests measure the talent they—and society—want. And he quotes from Riesman, lawyer and sociologist: "If people are underprepared for tests, they will generally be underprepared for courses" (ibid.). One must assume that, at least nowadays, universities want people with the best symbolic skills, not necessarily from the best social circles, although the two overlap.

Zigler (1978) adopts the procedure of staying with Head Start in the hope that better investigations will show its effectiveness. "Let us remember Head Start is America's national laboratory for testing and refining our efforts to improve the quality of the lives of our country's children" (p. 74). He had promoted the idea of Head Start in 1964-65, was the first director of the Office of Child Development, the "public servant, responsible for the administration of the program" (p. 71) affecting 350,000 children. The Nixon administration attempted to cut its $400 million budget because of the many empirical demonstrations that Head Start programmes had no value, but it was fought for and saved by "social activists," although, as Hodgson (1980, p. 107) shows, the main opposition to Nixon came from his civil servants who had been responsible for administering the programme. Zigler declares Head Start to be his "most important professional act" (p. 70) and, like the civil servants, he is unwilling to see it buried as a failure.

He offers three arguments in favour of its prolongation. First, he lists 9 projects carried out since 1974 and begun after the attempted scotching of the project by the Nixon administration. Although this "new evidence"—presumably the "old evidence," regarded by Cronbach (1975) and others as failing to show that Head Start had any long-term academic effects, was not quite up to the psychometric mark—is touted by Zigler as showing that Head Start children made more lasting gains than control children (p. 73), nevertheless there are problems. Having decided that the failure of the old Head Start programme was "an indictment of schools rather than Head Start" (p. 72), Zigler formed his own "follow through" (FT) programme for "economically disadvantaged" students in which classes of no more than 20 youngsters were tutored from kindergarten to the third grade (Abelson, Zigler and DeBlasi, 1974, p. 758). Little evidence of psychometric gains in standard and acceptable tests is to be seen in the longitudinal part of this study. The number of students was small (FT=35, NFT=26), the students were not randomly assigned to either group, and the psychometric quality of many of the tests was unknown or dubious (Torrance's "creativity" measures, an Attitude Towards School questionnaire and a Self-Esteem Inventory, to name only a few). Again, of all the 26 measures, performance on only 7 favoured the FT group at the 1 percent level of significance; that on

9 academic tests showed no marked differences between the groups (p. 764). This is surprising in view of the fact that the FT children were given individual attention while NFT children were taught as a class (p. 759). The conclusion, "the findings at the end of third grade showed a consistent pattern of superior performance by FT over NFT children" (p. 767), is unconvincing backing for the academic value of preschool compensatory programmes like Head Start.

Second, having decided that the New Head Start programme is "effective," Zigler wants it broadened to include "non-poor" children and the longitudinal study of gains in areas other than formal schooling: "social competence" and "emotional-motivational development" which would be divided into (1) locus of control, (2) healthy and appropriate responsivity to adults, and (3) the development of a positive self-image (op. cit., p. 73). The puzzle here would be to get agreement about the definition and measurement of the terms. When these have been attempted, as in the "locus of control" studies, the results have been unimpressive. Moreover, inserting them into the curriculum would be difficult because they involve value judgments that are unlikely to be shared by most articulate and concerned parents.

Third, Zigler pays a great deal of attention to the medical benefits, potential and real, of a new Head Start. He talks about its provision of "nutritious meals" and "physical and mental health services" (p. 73), of free inoculation against major epidemics and (in the future) of an "accident-prevention program" (p. 76). And (again in the future) he wants it expanded to care for "the optimal development of every child in this country" (p. 76). That is, Zigler is trying to make Head Start centres into publicly-financed community agencies for child development, an idea which he must know goes against the grain of Americans who judge the value of such extended projects against the standard of the taxpayer's dollar. It is unfair of Zigler to argue that critics of Head Start have merely provided "ammunition to those in America who feel that expending money in an effort to improve the lives of economically disadvantaged children is a waste" (op. cit., p. 72). These critics stated—and Zigler's own work simply corroborates this point—that Head Start conferred no academic advantages on these children. Even Zigler has to agree that the only children to be helped are those "who can benefit maximally from the Head Start experience" (p. 74). One hopes that this would not exclude those who still require the medical benefits. Zigler's plea for funding beyond that set in 1965 to take inflation into account is not likely to be answered. Apart from the fact that government spending in the early 1980s is for military hardware rather than social services, Zigler knows that he is faced with an uninterested public; he speaks of the "notoriously limited attention span of the American people" (Zigler, 1976, p. 338). But this is not the most economical explanation. From the publication of the first researches into the academic value of some programmes, a series of running fights began among social scientists as to the accuracy of the findings and the adequacy and appropriateness of the research strategies and statistical analyses employed. This is how social intellectuals operate: results running counter to profoundly-held consensus ideas

—"progress" in this case—are instantly counterattacked and the resulting confusion means that media representatives leave the topic alone. The members of the black community do the same because, as Frady (1980) has observed, "blacks now make up an even larger proportion of the nation's destitute than they did at the close of the Sixties" (p.15).

Despite this, social intellectuals continue their attempt to brighten up the picture. Darlington et al. (1980) followed up in 1976-1977 the performance of 1,599 mostly black youngsters ranging from 9 to 19 years and coming from 11 schools in which control and experimental groups were available. Since the original programmes and curricula were different, the only meaningful comparison was between groups and within schools (p. 202). Despite this, the investigators concentrate on results pooled from all the samples, a tactic which introduced another complexity. "To ensure that no single program accounted for a significant pooled result, we deleted the program with the strongest result from each analysis . . ." (p. 203). No information is given about the nature of the programmes omitted and the direction in which they were "strong." In any case, data from 5 of the 11 schools groups were dropped. The findings reported are also questionable. Information is not given about test-retest differences in the IQ scores. These are reported to be insignificant 3 or 4 years after "1 year of enrichment" (ibid.), from which the conclusion is drawn that "12 years of enriched schooling might have lifelong effects" (ibid.). The practical and logical problems associated with that inference are considerable.

Darlington and his associates are also interested in "failure to meet the school's basic requirements," a variable consisting of never being placed in special education classes and never being retained in a grade. On the combined variable, the only one for which information is provided, 5 of the the 7 projects showed no significant differences between the experimental and control groups. The median difference was significant for all 7 projects and in favour of the experimental groups, but the mean difference, a more appropriate statistic because of heterogeneity of the percentages of retention for projects, is not significant. The remaining information dealing with the two subsidiary variables (in special education classes or retained in grades) can be dismissed because only significant levels for median differences are provided and because the number of projects analyzed varies from 6 to 8. All in all, not a bright showing for Head Start programmes that had been carefully designed; too little information given (data on achievement test performance and interviews with parents were omitted altogether), too many puzzling deletions of projects, and statistics used that supported the author's thesis.

Nowadays, with the strident protest of the 1960's gone and people aware that discrimination on behalf of minority groups means reciprocal discrimination against other groups, writers detached from the Jensen-Kamin scuffling are suggesting that greater attention should be paid to those most likely to benefit from advanced education—"gifted children," their early discovery and special education (Amiel, 1977; Maeroff, 1977), regardless of whether their superiority is a product of training or heredity (or both). The difficult contemporary social problems will be solved (if they are soluble within the contemporary economic and bureaucratic framework) by the industrious and the educated, not by the common run of men. As Robertson has remarked, "one thing we must not put up with (is) the proneness of our rulers to unload society's sins on the schools" (Robertson, 1969, p. 221).

C. Attacking Jencks

Jencks was difficult to deal with because his findings ran counter to the assumption of the liberal consensus that social change could be brought about by educational change and also because of his advocacy of direct social reform to reduce what he regarded as the unjustified inequalities in American society. In an attempted rebuttal of Jencks, Yinger and his associates (1977) reported a Middle Start programme devised in 1964 as an experiment in the educational enrichment of young adolescents. This method of changing school performance by way of "the larger setting" (p. 17), was regarded as superior to Jencks' reliance on the changing of the social system, "Attention to the support of significant others, to the value placed on education by critical reference groups, is clearly necessary" (p. 17). The four authors claim to have done this and offer their results as a tentative "proof" that attention directed towards improving academic effort will also decrease the spread of economic inequality (p. 107).

Their main treatment variable was a six weeks summer programme at Oberlin College for talented disadvantaged youngsters from nearby cities. This was accompanied by a follow-up programme encouraging the experimental group to take every opportunity to finish high school and go to college. Recommendations about each student were made by Oberlin staff to school counsellors"... to make sure that each pupil took the courses likely to promote maximum attainment. Often this meant assignment to the college-bound track. It meant also being helped to succeed in required courses; hence counsellors were apprised of any problems, and tutoring was arranged" (p. 26). This attention to academic matters was increased as participants in the six-week programmes came close to finishing high school. "Characteristics of college, financial aid, the necessary tests, application forms and recommendations were stressed" (p. 27).

All the follow-up activities in the "larger setting" such as the encouragement of parents' clubs were directed to tutoring or keeping "the goal of further education alive" (p.26). This is true also of the arrangements made by the College for participants in a given city and summer programme to go for trips, to attend concerts or ball games, see movies, hear talks or attend a party. It was all done to reinforce achievement in school and university (p. 27); the former "critical reference groups" were teachers, counsellors and parents, and no attention was paid to "individual needs and motives" beyond educational achievements. Would this "enrichment" by tutoring succeed?

Consider the experimental plan of prematching before random assignment. The youngsters in grades 7 and 8 were matched on eight variables; ethnicity, sex, class in school, city, school district, school within the district (with one exception), father's place in the household, and academic and intelligence measures, and then were randomly assigned to the experimental and control groups (p. 37). The dependent variables centred on educational achievement: persistence in school (from completed tenth grade to entry to institutions of higher education): how long they spend in a special academic programme; whether they had, or had not, gone to private or special academic school; performance in achievement tests and in junior high and serious high grades (p. 54). Data are provided for years 1964, 1965 and 1966 (p. 51). The possibility that the groups would do better just because attention was being paid to them (the Hawthorne effect) is considered by the authors (pp. 103-104) but assumed to have no effect despite the saliency of the experimental students (special counselling and tutoring).

Statistical looseness shows up in a use of levels of confidence (about the chance nature of the differences between the experimental and control groups) that are less than stringent. For example, if the 10 per cent and five per cent levels of confidence are rejected, we find that, for 10 possible combinations of subjects in the two groups on the four dependent variables, 34 of the 40 were insignificant; if the five per cent level alone is accepted, that number decreases to only 25. Although the latter figure represents a greater-than-chance number of significant differences (eight out of 40), it is not, as the authors claim, a vote of confidence in their experimental treatment (p. 99).

They are especially happy with the marked differences between experimental and control performance, summed over the three years (1964, 1965, 1966), in point of four of the five dependent variables. However, the programme had not effect on Persistence in School, a curious and unexplained finding. Moreover, a breakdown of this total sample into subsamples shows that, of the other 40 differences (eight subsamples x five dependent variables), only eight are significant at the five per cent level or better (p. 102). Even the males, upon whom much attention was lavished (p. 30), could muster only two differences significant below the five per cent level. At best this means that the tutoring and guiding of talented but disadvantaged youngsters can result in academic performance that is superior to a comparable untutored group—scarcely an unusual finding. A cooler view would be that, despite a very intensive programme of coaching with potentially able students, a programme possibly aided by the Hawthorne effect, surprisingly little change occurred in the performance of most subsamples (p. 102). This is consistent with the finding, placed in an appendix at the end of the book, that by 1973 there were no marked differences between the percentages of the members of the experimental and control group who attended any institutions of higher education, even one labelled "select four-year college" (p. 118). Of the six other longitudinal comparisons made between the experimental and control group with respect to "attendance at a four-year institution" (p. 117), only three were significant at the five per cent level. After the intensive tutoring programme, these findings are a disappointment and lend indirect support to the idea implicit in Jencks, that experimental intervention in a "marginal institution" like the school has minimal effect.

Jencks has been more sharply attacked by Moynihan (1975) who points out that between 1962 and 1972 the increase in expenditures on education has been twice that of the GNP—indeed, $468 billion was spent on education in 1972 (Moynihan, 1975, p. 29)—and that "after a point expenditure does not seem to have any influence on school achievement" (p. 100). Any regional, class, racial and ethnic differences in school achievement will not be reduced by spending more money to achieve marginal gains (p. 114). One explanation of this state of affairs is given by Hearnshaw (1979) who argues cogently that quantitative genetics, which partitions the variance of the attribute in question into genetic and environmental components, is inapplicable to psychological functions which, instead of merely coping with the environment, processes information selectively picked up from it. "The difficulty is that the environment for human beings is not merely physical, but cultural, not merely the here and now, but historical, and culture and history become internalised in a way that renders them no longer merely environmental" (p. 62).

It is a fair guess that the children of poorer parents learn merely to cope with the day-to-day demands of the educational environment and that the use of symbolic skills for its "internalization" is characteristic of Jencks' more affluent parents whose children perform more effectively in school. The point has been made by Linestone (1973) in another context.

> A bitter lesson which every forecaster and planner learns is that the vast majority of his clientele has a very short planning horizon as well as a short memory. Most people are really only concerned about their immediate neighbourhood in space and occurrences which appear to be far removed from the present position are heavily discounted. Moreover, the degree of discounting may well vary with the individual's cultural and social status. A person at the bottom of Maslow's human values pyramid will discount environmental pollution much more heavily than someone near the top. The poor, for whom survival is a daily challenge are hardly going to lose much sleep over a pollution or population crisis twenty years in the future. A similar difference applies to space: a slum dweller worries about rats he can see, the jet set worries abut the depletion of wild game in distant Africa. . . . Americans seem to have a penchant for discounting. They are raised on installment buying and "fly-now-pay-later" exhortations (p. 335).

A more conspiratorial interpretation of Moynihan's position is given in Marceau's (1974) report that the children of parents in the "*classes populaires*" (manual workers of various degrees of skill, farmers and farm workers) are significantly under-represented in high schools (*lycées*), universities and especially in the "*Grandes Ecoles*," the most prestigious and specialized universities. In view of the relative absence of social mobility (Marceau, 1974, p. 222), Marceau believes that, somehow, the ruling classes, especially in metropolitan regions, consolidate their advantages by arranging for their children to enter the best schools and universities, obtain the best credentials and acquire the economic, social and cultural capital that sanctions their privileged position in the class structure (p. 207).

Dealing with British statistics, Halsey (1978) dallies with the same conspiratorial thesis. He indicates that, although 90 per cent of university graduates enter the professional and managerial classes (higher or lower), they represent only 37 per cent of all the entrants (Halsey, 1978, p. 127). The remaining youngsters in these classes have a selective (grammar-school) education coupled with some further non-university education. Halsey concludes that, although more secondary schools and universities were built in the 1950s and 1960s, the additional opportunities "have been seized disproportionately by those born into advantageous class circumstances" (p.130). The few workers' children who have attended state schools (elementary and comprehensive) and drifted into the upper two classes have assimilated the beliefs and values characteristic of the members of these classes, a process labelled "selective embourgeoisement" (p.134). Since then, the number of people with valid educational credentials required for better-paying jobs is small, and since these credentials and jobs will go overwhelmingly to the children of more affluent parents, equality of educational opportunity, let alone condition (a hypothetical state in which everybody has just about the same material advantages) "can never be attained through educational policies alone" (p. 135). In the current time of markedly increased unemployment and inflation unforseen by Halsey, his thesis still will be correct.

D. Credentialism and the Regnant Model

Thurow (1975) agrees with Moynihan, Halsey and Marceau that reliance on education "for curing all problems, economic and social, is unwarranted at best and in all probability ineffective" (Thurow, 1975, p. 184). His explanation, however, is quite different and requires for its understanding a summary of what Porter (1979) labels the old "regnant model" relating education and the acquisition of jobs.

The advances of industrialization and technology have brought with them a greatly-increased number of jobs requiring higher levels of education than formerly. This upgrading of the labor force has been achieved through the increased education which has accompanied industrial growth. Jobs themselves have increased educational content and jobs requiring higher levels of education have become a greater proportion of the total . . . with more and more education-loaded white-collar, service, brain work and less and less and educational-limited, blue-collar, goods-producing work (Porter, 1979, p. 263).

There has been an increase in the amount of education but Thurow would deny that it has any occupational value.

Speaking of the situation in the United States, he notes that in the relative affluence after 1945, jobs were readily available and employees had to take what schools and universities supplied (Hacker, 1970, p. 18). The fashionable "going to college" or taking some courses after high school changed lowly-skilled into highly-skilled ones with increasing wages (Thurow, 1975, p. 171). A greater number of years in schooling appeared to the working classes and the poor as the route to affluence for their children. In the 1970s, under the increasing momentum of automation, most jobs require only skills that can be learned on the job or some formal or informal training beyond high school. In the early 1970s, only 12 per cent of college graduates listed "formal training and specialized education as being useful for current work" (p. 176). Most people are over-schooled; beyond a number of basic skills in words and numbers, probably at about the grade 9 level, increased education is of little occupational value (Porter, 1979, p. 266). Examples of skills that can be learned on the job include those of bank tellers, key-punch operators, librarians, cooks, secretary-typists. Collins (1980) has even gone the length of arguing cogently, from an historical perspective, that only medicine, science and law are professions which require the expensive and time-consuming practice of attending University (for theory and knowledge—not for training of practical skills which are learned where they are used).

The upshot of all this is that, in educational terms, only three relatively homogeneous classes exist: those with a university degree (or its professional equivalent); those with some education after high school (electronic or mechanical technicians, nurses and military personnel) and those who receive training on the job (bus or truck drivers, sales persons, short-order cooks, bank-tellers and so on). Civil servants are difficult to fit into this scheme because they are varied in point of previous education and they are concentrated in certain geographical areas. This system of classification which has been found useful by Anderson (1980) is a barrier to people who see education as a means towards social mobility.

What is important now is what the economy demands, not what education supplies and, as far as higher education is concerned, the demand is for dentists, physicians, lawyers, linguists and some scientists and technologists who need advanced formal education (Thurow, p. 181). Entry into these professions requires credentials (diplomas and certificates) unattainable unless people are allowed into appropriate training because of a suitable performance on tests which may be poorly related to career competence. Such screening tests, of which LSAT is an example, are used for promotional purposes (in police work, for example) as well as for entering selective professions. These credentials, presenting special problems for poorer people, create an inequality which is more rigid than ever before because the relatively affluent go to good schools which prepare them to acquire good credentials whereas poorer people have no such advantage.

If, then, the functional connection between social mobility (occupational status) and the amount of education has been largely severed, how can psychologists who were largely responsible for forging that link in the first place, defend their own demand for credentials?

6 / THE CREDENTIALS OF PSYCHOLOGY AS A SCIENCE

Before the dismal record of psychology as putative science of some sort is listed, a resumé of some previous comments on this topic is in order. Psychological science may belong to one of two categories. First, there is Science 1, a natural science in which causal (or conditional) laws are sought by the experimental manipulation and observation of physical variables. Second, the more disreputable Science 2 is characterized by probabilistic laws arrived at by correlational methods. It should be clear by now that psychology in general cannot be included in Science 1; its claim to this status rests mainly on behaviouristic studies of infra-human organisms in which the experimental setting is so restricted that the organisms can perform only the behaviour that is expected of them. This is a pathetic model of the human situation, athough it must be admitted that some people are only passive objects (retardates, seniles) to whom some Science 1 formulations might apply well enough.

Despite their use of experimental methods to manipulate cognitive functions, cognitive psychologists, even more obviously, cannot be included as exponents of Science 1 for two reasons. First, they do not subscribe to the idea that the organism is relatively passive; on the contrary, they assume that the organism is actively searching for information for adaptive purposes (Bruner and Olver, 1963, pp. 125-126). Second, without a commonly-accepted theoretical structure relating conceptual, memorial and motivational concepts, they cannot follow the practice of the natural scientists who control all variables except one which is systematically varied and a change in the dependent variable recorded (Petronovitch, 1979), a point noted by McGuire (1973, p. 447) and Park (1976, p. 104). The present contention, then, is that the methodological differences between behaviouristic and cognitive psychologists lies in the size of the measurement errors only. It is also assumed that the "laws" derived from behaviouristic studies are causal but quite useless for prediction and control in the world at large;

cognitive laws, on the other hand, are only of a probabilistic sort requiring the use of causal inferences for purposes of interpretation. Cattell (1966) has put this point rather well.

> The indispensable basis for causal inference is not manipulation but evidence for certain invariable sequential patterns established in the events observed. Evidence of this kind happens to come very readily as an accompaniment of manipulation, but manipulation itself is not part of the requirement (p. 8).

For example, from Milgram's (1974) report of his many experimental investigations into the conditions promoting what he labelled "obedience to authority," the only conclusions that can be drawn is his finding of a relationship between two variables: varying instructions to the subject to carry out the task (punishing the victim) and the extent of the "shock" they inflicted. Milgram's conclusion that he has provided evidence for "obedience to authority" is an inference, and not the only one possible (Mixon, 1974, p. 80).

Correlational analyses, eked out by causal inferences of this sort, are flawed in many ways. Apart from the undergraduate criticisms that they do not imply causation, there is the unhappy fact that in simple or more complex (multivariate) forms they have achieved nothing but squabbling among experts. Again, their use violates at least some of the conditions which made them originally applicable to non-psychological data (Detterman, 1979, p. 166-167). Moreover, they refer to a standard situation in a given milieu, not what people are potentially capable of doing in changed circumstances. Again, in critical situtations like Head Start, there is never an agreement except among friends about the correct statistic to use (Cohen and Garet, 1975). Finally, even a very stable correlation—that between IQ and socio-economic status, for example—can be interpreted very differently (Firkowska, 1973; Jensen, 1972, pp. 153-154). Despite this, cognitive psychologists often pretend that they are Science 1 psychologists searching for conditional laws; at worst, their findings are unstable; at best they are of a probabilistic sort which can be interpreted in different ways.

Recent surveys of the empirical record of psychology as a science reveal only its ersatz quality which is not confined to any one of its formal subdivisions.

A. Experimental Psychology

General and experimental psychologists have championed disparate and competing theories to a degree that is unknown in the theoretically more coherent physical and biological sciences (Koch, 1974, p. 24) and have often tied themselves to laboratory phenomena about which they have no secure interpretations (Allport, 1975). Even Skinner (1953; 1971; 1974) nods. Worrisome is the marked change in his theories over time (Dennett, 1978; Mills, 1978 a; 1978 b; Herrenstein, 1977 a). For example, determinism, prediction and control were always a feature of Skinner's formulations (Skinner, 1953, pp. 6, 14) until recently (Skinner, 1974, p. 21). Again, "genetic endowment," discounted by Skinner in 1953 as a formative influence on behaviour, is accepted in 1974 (p. 188), and some former colleagues have now agreed about the scientific respectability of cognitive variables like "consciousness," "expectation," and "self" (Bandura, 1977a).

B. Social Psychology

Social psychologists are also concerned about their lack of contribution to psychology as a science and to the solution of social problems (Elms, 1975). For example, Silverman (1978), dealing with studies investigating the influence of violence in the media—scarcely a problem of great magnitude now (Constantineau, 1978)—comments on social psychologists' "short-term, low impact experiments yielding an array of inconsistent and contradictory results . . ." (Silverman, 1978, p. 356). In an elegant paper McGuire (1973) admits these defects. He traces them to the use of the hypothetico-deductive method beloved by Science 1 social psychologists, and to their desire to support any hypotheses in which they have invested time and money, a desire that is usually satisfied if they face data (printouts) rather than people. Working against Silverman, Aron (1979) has argued that social pscyhologists should discover "the principles by which individuals (even a few) can restructure social conditions . . ." (Aron, 1979, p. 50) so that "hindrances to adequate functioning" such as "improving general physical health, raising the overall resistance to stress . . ." can be eliminated. Unfortunately, such a programme rests on a misconception, salient during the 1960s, of the nature of society—that society exercises a control over the individual that can be changed by psychological study and action (Bandura, 1974). Aron's belief that the individual must change society because the reverse situation implies totalitarianism runs against the fact the the large corporations have their own planning system that exercises a flexible, powerful and hidden control over people which is more than a match for any social psychologist's attempt at consciousness raising.

C. Developmental Psychology

There have been no breakthroughs in developmental psychology, "for the problems on which society wants help are ones that represent massive difficulties in the relationship between people . . . or between individuals and the social system . . ." (Sears, l975, p. 67). Even Piaget, whose longevity, productivity and general intellectual skills have allowed him to shake off cogent early critics like Hazlitt (l930), is now under heavy siege (Siegel and Brainerd, 1978) and has admitted that his developmental theorizing has a more restricted range of applicability than he had earlier claimed (Piaget, 1972). An iconoclast like Sears is reduced to believing that cumulative research during the last 50 years supporting praise rather than punishment has resulted in a "widespread increase in children's liking for schoolwork and in their achievement" (p. 67). Unsurprisingly, no evidence for this is cited. Again, Sears goes the length of supporting "categorically" the idea that a child deprived of parental affection between 6 months and 2 years will grow up to be irreversibly harmed in some way as an adult (p. 68). Unfortunately for most developmental psychologists, this idea that nourished them for many years is now known to be untrue (Clarke and Clarke, 1976). To people who argue that parents have brought up children very well in the past without any help from psychologists, the counter has always been that things would have gone better with a dash of the science of developmental psychology. Such a riposte is no longer possible.

D. Affective Psychology

The bewildering number of personality theories and concepts, and the unstable findings place this topic beyond the range of a scientific subdiscipline (Phares and Lamiell, 1977, p. 133). Psychotherapy is in a similar situation (Drummond, 1980); its one stable finding, the significant and sizeable reationship between social class and mental illness of all sorts, has been ignored by most salient theorists. Behaviour therapies no longer enjoy their favourable press (Lazarus, 1976). Certainly behaviour modification therapy has been much more successful than any of its rivals. However no one knows why it is successful; is it simply the administration of the reinforcer or is it the person's expectation of reinforcement (Bandura, 1977b) or is it the reinforcing model, usually described in non-Skinnerian terms?

Indeed, the whole concept of "mental illness" is suspect. The "medical model" of this illness has been indicted by Sarbin (1967) because of the fallacious logic on which it is based. Amusing examples have been recorded of the conceptually fragile but politically potent diagnostic repertoire of clinicians. For example, Rosenhan (1973) reports some observations made by eight normal people who gained admittance to twelve psychiatric hospitals of various sorts by pretending to hear noises. Diagnosed as schizophrenic, they behaved normally in the hospitals for an average of 19 days. They discovered that their fellow patients were better able to detect their sanity than the staff whose perception of the pseudopatients' behaviour was shaped by the diagnostic label. They also found that, on discharge, the label persisted and they were declared to be "in remission" of their schizophrenia. Informed of these findings, the staff members of another hospital doubted whether Rosenhan could slip through more pseudopatients. A significant decrease in admissions to that hospital followed, although he never repeated the stunt. Since "mental illness" is declared to be present when behaviour is seen to deviate from certain psychosocial, ethical or legal norms, it is reasonable to assume that much of the work of clinical staff is to "warehouse" people, who are a nuisance to the existing social order (Hurvitz, 1973, p. 235).

E. Educational Psychology and Research

Educational psychology and research, long regarded in North America as the vehicle for social change (Ladd, 1894, p. 19), comprise a disaster area.

Grinder (1978) remarks that "Educational psychology... is a reality of irreconcilable differences" (1978, p. 289) and Jackson (1978) is as upset about educational research. In fact educational policy is never established or changed as a result of psychological contributions or any other empirical research, because policy in the form of ideas consists of selected information "given meaning and charged with social purpose by larger ideas, assumptions and political judgements which are not empirical in nature" (Cohen and Garet, 1975, p. 21). Why, then, do Koch's "sub-cartels of knowledge" not merely survive but actually thrive? Two factors are worth considering because they have sustained the need for credentials in psychology, especially with respect to the acquisition of information about sophisticated but useless methodology, and have somehow made people forget that psychology has promised much but delivered little.

7 / DEFENCE MECHANISMS

Psychological Scientists have fought tough rearguard actions against critics, using a variety of tactics.

A. Institutional Forces

First consider the momentum of a large organized group of conventionally-trained psychologists who are not about to admit that their training is theoretically or professionally pointless. Their number increased greatly after the Second World War when they accepted the role of social technocrats, potentially capable of solving social problems as successfully as scientists and technologists dealt with inanimate matter (Hodgson, 1976, p. 76). The sudden flow of research grants had unfortunate consequences, principal among which is the fact that once a body of social knowledge has been established, falsification, however justified, becomes difficult because editors and their consultants often turn aside negative results in order to protect bodies of findings and interpretations in which they have a vested interest (Cartwright, 1973, p. 229; Entwhistle, 1972, p. 385). The result is that researchers, whose fame depends on the quantity of their publications, tend to choose the sample, the data and the conditions of the experiment so that they are spared the embarrassment of reporting negative results (McGuire, 1972, p. 449) which are almost certain to be rejected.

B. Authoritative Voices

A second reason for the continued existence of sub-cartels of psychological knowledge is the presence of authoritative voices reminding psychologists that they are committed to the establishment of a "pure science" of behaviour providing laws from which they can derive explanations of extra-laboratory phenomena. For example, Atkinson (1972) concentrates on our role as scientists: ". . . the psychologist's job as a scientist is to search for data, principles and laws that enlarge our understanding of psychological phenomena" (Atkinson, 1977, p. 207). The problem is: whose data, whose principles, whose laws? Atkinson, and Hebb (1974) are reduced to producing lists of findings and theories which are very different but equally uncompelling. McLeish's (1963) plan is to award favourite psychologists the same status as that occupied by eminent natural scientists. In his salad days he considered Pavlov as "one of the great figures of world science" (McLeish, 1962, p. 185), on a plane with Newton and Darwin (p. 184). He regarded it as highly "unlikely that a crucial experiment will falsify such a theory . . ." (p. 193), forgetting the work of Zener (1937) who showed that a conditioned dog will, if unharnessed, cease to salivate on the presentation of the conditioned stimulus and will move towards the pan in which its food was normally kept. There is also the fact that Pavlov's theory of brain functioning is incorrect—indeed was at odds with what was known of neurophysiology in Pavlov's own day (Gray, 1979, pp. 102-103). What appears to have led McLeish astray is his perception of psychology as a science that would incorporate economically "thousands of (presumably stable) empirical observations about the behaviour of animals and human beings" (McLeish, 1963, p. 193), rather than as a way of understanding and possibly helping people.

Not surprisingly McLeish's contemporary hero is Skinner, "the most eminent psychologist at the present time" (McLeish, 1976, p. 70) and on a par with Newton (p. 69). According to McLeish, Skinner "seeks to improve human action by a revised structure of society based on a rational system of rewards and punishment" (p. 81). However, Platt's (1973) much modified Skinnerian plan to reach that goal is not even plausible on paper because of his refusal to take into account the barrier of social (mainly economic) forces. If, with Petronovich (1979) we see much of psychology as "behaviour in a context" (p. 373), then an account must be given of the significant variables in that context and Skinner and his associates fail to do that. McLeish's dilemma is understandable. He contends that in the long run "the scientific picture of the universe is simpler, easier to understand, is more general in its content—than any other picture" (1965, p. 5). This is true but it does not mean that the study of people, whose predilection for making value-judgments makes them substantially different from the material "universe," will become part of this "scientific picture," Science 1.

Some bold psychologists, ignoring past failures, have declared that the profession could help make desirable social changes—of course through personal efforts. This line of thinking appeared in Bandura's (1974) Presidential Address to the American Psychological Association. There he assumed, wrongly as it has turned out, that North Americans recognize the necessity for making changes. "With growing populations and spread of lavish life-styles taxing finite resources, people will have to learn to cope with new realities of human existence" (p. 869). Accordingly, "Psychology . . . can provide (people) with the means for effecting personal and social change. And it can aid them in making making value-choices by assessing the consequences of alternative life-styles and institutional arrangements" (p. 869).

This is unlikely to be true. A more accurate assertion is that only the wealthy can make "personal changes" (Schur, 1976, pp. 90-91), and there is no evidence that these are necessarily of the ascetic sort required by Bandura. For the vast majority of the community, changes in "life styles" are engineered, because they are likely to be profitable, by the hirelings of corporations, the wealth of which stems from consumption and buying. This is a commonplace notion understood by interested amateurs. Why did it elude Bandura in 1973? Why did he ignore the fact that there exist powerful groups in society which control people by promoting the priorities of an economic system that are incompatible with prosocial behaviour in the form of the satisfaction of common human needs for jobs, adequate housing, clean air and a cheap and efficient medical service? We must presume ignorance arising from professional deformation.

Aware of the fact that his earlier assumption of the passivity of the subject in the face of environmental pressures (Bandura and Walters, 1962) was unrealistic if that same subject were to take an active part in changing himself and society, Bandura had begun in the late 1960s to trade in his old model for a new cognitive, information-processing one which has informed his later work (Bandura, 1977a). For example, reinforcers, he argues, are not the only determinants of behaviour. The consequences of a response often provide information (feedback via reafferent stimuli) about the appropriateness of the responses. This is Platt's (1973) position but, unlike Platt, Bandura talks about this behavioural accommodation in terms of the "intervening influence of thought" (1974, p. 860). Again, people can motivate themselves by working out future outcomes symbolically so that their behaviour may bring them "anticipated benefits" and allow them to "avert future trouble" (p. 860). Specifically, people may use favourable outcomes, based on realistic expections, to direct their behaviour. Accordingly, Bandura concludes that the "consumptive life-styles" which threaten man's chance of survival (he forgets nuclear war and the widespread trade in conventional weapons) will be laid aside. "The information-processing capacities with which humans are endowed provide the basis for insightful behaviour. Their capacity to bring remote consequences to bear on current behaviour by anticipatory thought supports foresightful action" (ibid.).

Criticisms of these ideas have been made before but are worth repeating because they are often ignored. (a) The vast majority of people are not greatly concerned about "remote consequences." (b) Plumping for an "information-processing model" of human behaviour is a return to a popular paradigm which is quite useless until details about the information, its source and the nature of the processing are supplied. (c) The economic system, based on reliable and consistent spending by consumers, particularly on profitable items like automobiles, electronic gadgetry and clothes which must be regularly bought, repaired and discarded, cannot survive if people turn to ascetic living. More, since the manufacturers of these products depend for their sale on the mass media which also provide slanted national and international news as well as diverting models, it is most unlikely that "consumptive life-styles" will disappear because people make a decision to do so. For example, 1975-1976 was an excellent year for U.S.

automobiles which use excessive amounts of a depleting resource like gasoline and emit large quantities of tailpipe poisons. The fact that comfort was more important than ecological considerations was reflected also in the reciprocal decline in the sale of "compacts" and "subcompacts" (Asbell, 1976). The automobile unit most popular in the 1977 model year was a Ford pick-up truck getting low mileage per gallon. This state of affairs has now changed, with some help from the recession, but there is no reason to suppose that the general expectations of plenty generated by forty years of affluence will be dissipated easily.

Bandura (1978) has presented a methodological justification of his position that there are processes by which people can control their own behaviour. Labelled "reciprocal determinism," it refers to the fact that, potentially at least, behaviour, cognitions and the environment mutually interact as cause and effect (p. 345). The cognitions (self-observation, judgmental process and self response) are complex (p. 349) and amount to a self-generated reward which is handy when an individual wants to get his weight down or perform better at university (p. 353). It is interesting to note that the experiments cited by Bandura in support of this deal with minor matters within the control of the individual; indeed "locus of control" turns out to be one of the "judgmental" processes. In larger areas of social life like the recent strike of U.S. coalminers, it is difficult to see how fragile notions like self-generated reward can possibly be of any explanatory value (Caudill, 1978).

Bandura assumes that people will change, helped by the psychologist, because they are close to intolerable conditions. Sperry (1977) is unwilling to wait for changes to take place until "the margin of tolerability" (p. 238) is reached. Aided by some agile verbal hat-tricks, he argues that the brain uses a mixture of facts and values ("subjective experience") to guide behaviour. He writes sentences like these:

> The causal power attributed to the subjective properties resides in the hierarchical organization of the nervous system and in the power exerted by any whole over its parts. . . . Subjective experience in the present scheme is put to work in brain function and gives a reason for being and for having been involved in a physical system (Sperry, 1977, p. 239).

Sperry seems to be arguing that because the mind-brain has a causal status and because "the whole value-rich qualitative world of inner, conscious, subjective experiences (the world of the humanities), which has long been explicitly excluded from the domain of science on behaviourist-materialist principles, becomes reinstated" (pp. 239-249), then "the world view of science, and hence the kinds of human values supported by science, are greatly altered in humanistic quality" (p. 240).

What are these values that are acceptable to science? Here Sperry becomes understandably very abstract and cautious: ". . . what is good, right, or to be valued is defined very broadly to be that which accords, sustains, and enhances the orderly design of evolving nature . . . with special focus on evolution in our own biosphere" (p. 243). Without giving any examples of how these values are to be realized, Sperry contends that they can overturn conditions like poverty, pollution and overpopulation if only—how again he does not specify—they can be got, even vaguely, into the heads of ordinary people (p. 237).

One weakness of Sperry's postion is his assumption that, since poverty, pollution and overpopulation reflect "man-made" values, they can be altered (scientifically) by superior "man-made values." However, the important question revolves around the term "man-made." In fact, poverty and the like are the product of an economic system the target of which is to accumulate wealth for its beneficiaries to the disadvantage of many who lack sizeable amounts of inherited capital or appropriate talents. People in management or in "technostructure" who try to pursue any other goal with some intensity are rapidly eliminated. Accordingly, poverty and so on are "system-made" and, since men of talent, whose work contributes to this goal of profit-making, are unlikely to turn against it, powerful people with superior "man-made" values are more a refurbished dream of the 1960s (Marcuse, 1969, pp. 27-28) than a realistic prediction of likely events in the near future.

It would be unwise, of course, to exculpate people from this state of affairs. The "system-made" values such as the aggressive pursuit of material advantages, the envy of those superior in this sense and the dislike of those inferior, the overwhelming selfishness, must be accepted, or at least tolerated, by the vast mass of people (Friedenburg, 1976). For example, Hodgson (1976) points out that poorer people in America do not hate the rich; they envy them. "The ultimate hero of blue-collar America is perhaps . . . Sinatra. Looking at a . . . Sinatra, the ordinary American is looking at a big winner in the lottery in which he also believes that he owns a ticket" (Hodgson, 1976, p. 489). This illusion is backed by gambling, lotteries and media money games (and misinformation). Just how long this process of mystification will continue to be successful is as difficult to predict as the outcome of its failure.

An even weaker assumption by Sperry (1972) is that a scientifically sound and coherent value/belief system stems from the axiom that "the grand design that created man, with special focus on evolution in our own biosphere, is something intrinsically good that is right to preserve and enhance, and wrong to destroy or degrade" (p. 120). This is nonsense; if it were true, we would not be in the mess from which Sperry is trying to extricate us with his conceptual manoeuvering bereft of evidence. A more likely speculation is that consciousness and its intellectual functions, forcing the environment to meet its demands, seems to have partly extricated people from the evolutionary process to the detriment of themselves and many associated species. "Man has already furthered evolution very considerably, half unconsciously, and for his own advantages . . ." (Galton, 1883, p. 198). But even Galton believed that man "might devote his modicum of power, intelligence and kindly feelings to render its (evolution's) future progress less slow and painful" (ibid.). The assumption that people are guided by reason and "kindly feelings" is more honourable than realistic.

Psychologists are never more sure of themselves than when they find apparent cerebral bases for the psychological functions they are studying.

This is the old tactic of trying to make psychology a science by shifting it close to a genuine science, in this case neurophysiology. For example, Das, Kirby and Jarman (1975) claim that Luria, the late Russian psychophysiologist, has anchored two processes, simultaneous and successive scanning (synthesis) to a physiological substrate which is somehow (the mechanism is not specified) the product of experience and training (p. 88). This is a useful substitute (provided nobody realizes that it raises the mind-body problem) for Jensen's more openly-controversial ability notions, and it is important to examine the strategy in terms of which the three authors set about finding data to "confirm" Luria's neurologically based speculation.

The first problem is the relationship between "processes, abilities and behaviour." In the abstract of their paper, processes are said to underlie "abilities," the position adopted by Estes. But the first paragraph of the paper contains the following remark. "One of the apparent advantages of considering processes is their proximity to behaviour or performance" (p. 87). The authors are unclear about the relationship among the three terms although it is central to their enquiry. Again, in the same paragraph, the argument is advanced that "it is easier and more meaningful to integrate the interplay between genetic endowments," past experience and the nature of the task by a resort to "processes" rather than "abilities." Why? This was certainly never the case in the past when the use of the term "abilities" was more widespread and the educational performance of children not inferior. Specifically, if a person has a high ability in mathematics, it would be reflected in his school performance and later tasks which required such an ability. It is difficult to understand why a substitute label should be of any advantage in this context except as a popular professional euphemism. Later in their paper, Das, Kirby and Jarman speculate that the "quality" of intellectual performance is best explained in terms of either of the two processes (simultaneous or successive) at work within the boundary of the "ability" in question. Paivio (1976) points out that the use of "ability" or "process" is just a matter of labelling, but this fine semantic distinction point is fairly important for the three authors.

They pursue their tactic of denigrating the unwanted notion of "ability." First, they associate it with the "conceptual ghosts" of the long-obsolete "faculty psychology," despite the fact that a "process" inferred from behaviour is just as much a "ghost" as any cognitive function like an ability (pp. 87-88). Then they look askance at the supposed physiological basis formerly attached to "ability" psychology, i.e., that the left cortical hemisphere is the substrate of "verbal ability" and the right hemisphere of nonverbal reasoning and spatial ability. Against this psychological parallel, the authors present two arguments: (a) that the verbal "output" cannot be predicted by the physiological structure, and (b) "excellence in verbal ability . . . has not been identified with excellence in the structure itself" (p. 88).

There are several answers to these points: (a) Well-known "ability" psychologists arrived at their conclusions using a statistical technique different from that of the physiologist, and published their work before the findings of Sperry's split-brain technique became popularly known in the early 1960s (in Blakemore, 1977, p. 159); (b) It is difficult to know how one could make predictions from the physiological structure beyond the fact that significant damage to it results in appropriate disability. As Sperry (1968) points out, the two intact hemispheres collaborate during most mental tasks, one hemisphere being only relatively more active than the other. (c) "Verbal ability" is a category that refers to all kinds of verbal performance. For example, Hutt (1972) reports studies showing that females are markedly superior to males in the executive aspects of language (spelling, punctuation, fluency, writing) but not in verbal reasoning or comprehension. (d) The word "excellence" is being used in two different senses. "Excellent verbal abilities" can be observed and measured, but this is not yet true of the physiological substrate. As a result, no parallel between excellence in the two domains is possible unless it is taken to mean the relationship between physiological damage and learning deficits, a point not mentioned by the authors.

Das, Kirby and Jarman proceed to present their account of Luria's (1973) physiological orientation to information processing. The brain is divided into three functional units: for arousal and attention, for input recoding and storage, and for planning and programming behaviour. Sensory integration is carried out by the second of these units, located in the occipital, parietal and fronto-temporal regions. On the basis of his observations of cortical lesions in different brain locations, Luria suggested two major methods of information processing—simultaneous and successive. The choice of which method to be used is declared to be determined by: "(a) the individual's habitual mode of processing information as determined by socio-cultural and genetic factors, and (b) the demands of the task" (p. 91). Simultaneous processing of information requires the organization of input into groups so that the relationships of parts to the whole can be grasped and manipulated; these wholes are often, but not necessarily, spatially organized. Successive processing involves the arrangements of stimuli into a sequence or serial order, each piece of information being connected by cues to all the other pieces; this factor is temporally organized. Luria has observed that damage to fronto-temporal regions results in disturbance to successive processing, while lesions in the occipito-parietal area result in deficits in simultaneous processing.

There are various problems associated with the attempt of Das, Kirby and Jarman to explore the invariance of simultaneous-successive processing across IQ groups, age groups, socio-economic classes and cultures. The first is the fact that Das's model will tend to be "confirmed" by factor analysis because his matrix consists of two groups of tests known to show high within-group and low between-group correlations. Specifically, tests with a heavy spatial loading were chosen as markers for simultaneous processing (Progressive Matrices, Figure Copying, Memory for Designs, Cross-modal Coding), whereas Serial and Free Recall, the markers for successive processing, are substantially verbal. Of the latter, Vernon, Ryba and Lang (1978, p. 4) remark that their close similarity "tends to yield a spurious factor . . . which provides the main basis for Das' successive processing" (p. 4). Given this and the notorious orthogonality of the spatial (simultaneous) and verbal (successive) factors (Vernon, 1970), it is not surprising that Das' two factors emerge in most of his investigations in which tests measuring these items are used.

Moreover, if this criticism is true, it may be predicted that, when any verbal test is introduced into the matrix of intercorrelations among tests of simultaneous and successive scanning, it will load on the successive factor, and reciprocally a nonverbal test associated with spatial ability will load on the simultaneous factor (p. 94). Again, when a similarities test, largely of a verbal nature (stating how pairs of nouns are alike), is assumed to be a test of "simultaneous synthesis" because it "involves the grasping of superordinate relationships" (p. 95), it will have a moderate loading on the successive factor (p. 96).

Another problem the authors face is the replacement of "the usual division of abilities into reasoning and memory" (p. 92) with their two scanning modes. For example, Raven's Progressive Matrices is usually listed as a measure of relatively "culture-fair" general intelligence (Jensen, 1972, p. 78) or capacity for conceptual learning and abstract thinking (p. 194), a point Das, Kirby and Jarman do not deny (1975, p. 92). However, after it loads highly, but not uniquely, on the simultaneous factor, it becomes a marker for that factor. So do Memory for Designs and Cross-modal Coding (recognizing which of three dot patterns resemble visual stimuli), neither of which has ever been shown to measure simultaneous scanning—the authors admit this with respect to the first test—but both do have some face validity in the sense that they regularly load heavily on the simultaneous factor.

But there is a surprising number of anomalous loadings. In the first study in which the two sorts of tests were administered to 60 retarded and 60 non-retarded children, Memory for Designs loaded heavily on the Simultaneous factor for non-retarded children and on the Successive factor for retardates, and Cross-modal Coding and Visual Short-term Memory also showed anomalous (and unexplained) loadings (p. 92). In another study exploring information processing in relation to age and socio-economic status, the test battery, expanded to include Figure Copying, Word Reading and Colour Naming, was given to samples of six and ten year-old children. Three factors, the famous two plus a speed factor, emerged. The Visual Short-term Memory task loaded anomalously on the successive factor for the older children and on the speed factor for the younger children. Further the same three factors emerged when the same battery was given to 60 low socio-economic status children and to 60 of their more affluent counterparts. Again, disparities appeared. Visual Short-term Memory loaded on successive and speed factors for both groups, while Cross-modal Coding had moderate or high loadings on all factors for both groups, with the exception of high SES children on the successive factor.

However, the most anomalous loadings are to be found when a different test battery was administered to Edmonton children of high and low socio-economic status and high-caste rich and poor children in Orissa, India. In the Orissa study the tasks administered were Progressive Matrices,

Figure Copying, Memory for Designs, Cross-modal Coding, Visual Short-term Memory and Word Reading. The Edmonton study included as well IQ measures from school records, Serial and Free Recall tests and scores in Mathematics and Reading achievement. Anomalous loadings were observed for the Progressive Matrices (high on the successive factor for Edmonton children, but on both factors for the Orissa children); for Cross-modal Coding (a high loading on speed for the Orissa children and a substantial loading on all factors except speed in the Edmonton sample), and for Visual Short-term Memory (loadings on the successive factor for the Orissa sample, and on successive and speed for the Edmonton sample). It should also be pointed out that, for the latter sample, IQ, Serial Recall and Free Recall loaded on both factors, and that Word Reading had a negative loading on the achievement factor (p. 94). Finally, in "an exploratory" factor analysis of eleven variables in which the two factors contributed only 39 percent of the total variance, only five tests supported the predictions unequivocally while three tests falsified the predictions (p. 96).

Das, Kirby and Jarman (1975) also report comparative patterns of cognitive abilities in native children living on an Alberta reserve after the teaching of largely the sequential processing of information to low achieving students in grades 3 and 4. Some anomalous findings are worth recording. (a) After the intervention programme in which use of sequential processing was taught, the loadings on Raven's Progressive Matrices changed in the wrong direction: before intervention, they were .678 (successive) and .458 (simultaneous) while afterwards they were .253 and .544, respectively. (b) Visual Short-term Memory loaded on the speed and simultaneous factors in the pretest, and similar but no high loadings on successive and simultaneous factors on the post-test (p. 97). (c) In terms of gain scores, one would expect to see a change in WISC verbal scores, but not in WISC performance. In fact, just the opposite occurred. (d) Analysis of variance of post-test comparisons between maximum and minimum treatment groups, defined in terms of hours of intervention, failed to show any significant differences except for the Serial Learning tasks, even after the dubious use of analysis of covariance to remove pre-test differences (Maguire and Haig, 1976). At best, these two factors appear, but they are not invariant across cultures and social classes in the sense that the tasks did not invariably load on the same factors.

There are two additional criticisms to be made of Das, Kirby and Jarman. The first, which relates especially to the later work of Jarman and Das (1977), is Carroll's (1979) point that the matrices of correlations used by Jarman and Das can be made to yield a general factor, which could be interpreted as "g," when subjected to a kind of factor analysis that is just as reputable (or disreputable) as any other sort. The second criticism is that the test batteries were designed to yield only their two factors. When the batteries included speed tests, highly intercorrelated but poorly correlated with marker tests for the two factors, a speed factor emerged (p. 93); an achievement factor appeared in the same way, and Vernon, Ryba and Lang (1978), using a much larger battery of tests and a sample of undergraduate students with a smaller within-group variance, discovered six "ability" factors (op. cit., p. 10). The additional tests "begin to splinter off into the familiar verbal, spatial and numerical factors to form the hierarchical taxonomy of mental abilities envisioned by Vernon, and to some extent the two-tier model proposed by Jensen" (Vernon, Ryba and Lang, 1978, p. 12).

This conclusion is at odds with Luria's notion that the higher mental functions are culturally determined: intelligence, that is, becomes "the use of information behaviour effectively for goal attainment" (p. 98). Although this is a great deal less dangerous as a position than turning to ability psychology and its hereditarian links, nevertheless it poses formidable problems for the understanding of retardation. The authors' escape route takes the form of speculation, argument and assertion. "Ability" becomes a boundary condition, defined in terms of cortical structure within which psychological processes operate:

> It is conceivable that normal and retarded individuals have basic differences in the substrate of their intellectual functions. But, since equivalent mental age should give an equivalent structural basis, a retarded child should be able to acquire the same large number of skills as a normal child, given sufficient training. . . . The equivalence of structure (mental age) implies an equivalence of ability, so the differences in performance must be understood in terms of the processes which the person uses. The processes used by a retarded person cannot be reduced to his abilities (p. 102).

This slippery passage is central to the paper by Das, Kirby and Jarman. Its weakness lies in the notion that "equivalent mental age" should "give an equivalent structural basis." Cortical structure, at least up to adolescence and possibly beyond, is more likely to be a developing state of affairs than a static boundary condition. This can be illustrated by introducing the notion of chronological age (CA): a retarded child with a mental age (MA) of six and a CA of eight differs markedly from a child with an MA of eight and a CA of six, as any teacher knows. Regardless of postulated similarities in "structural basis" between the two youngsters, the former child has fallen behind in functions such as information processing and the retrieval of memories, a lag that is almost certain to continue permanently. To put it another way, the boundaries of the retarded children restrict their processing and retrieval of information to a greater degree than those of their more gifted age-mates.

Two final comments are in order. While dealing with the relationship between simultaneous and successive scanning and reading, Cummins and Das (1977) state: "The simultaneous/successive model is especially useful because of the explicit neurological reference. Luria's observations have specified the cortical locations underlying different types of simultaneous and successive processes" (Cummins and Das 1977, 250). But Luria merely made inferences from brain-damaged patients, inferences that amount to poor psychological practice when they are used as a basis for explaining the working of the intact brain. As Gregory (1962) has demonstrated, ablation of part of the brain with accompanying deficits in psychological functions does not guarantee a functional brain-body relationship without a knowledge of how the entire cortical system and its interrelated and self-stabilizing parts are organized. Gregory remarks, "The general conclusion seems to be that where we know how a system works, the result of damage can be explained, but to deduce how the system works from the result of damage is extremely difficult" (Gregory, 1962, p. 25). This, however, is exactly what Luria has done.

There is also a logical problem that has emerged from this reliance on a neurological frame of reference. According to Cummins and Das, because Luria has specified a cortical substrate for his two psychological processes, "differences between reading disabled children and normal children in the relationship between simultaneous and successive dimensions and aspects of linguistic and reading performance can be explicitly related to underlying neurological phenomena" (ibid.). This is the logical fallacy: if A (material substrate), then B (S/S processes). Given B (the processes and their relationship to reading performance), then A. Cummins and Das make the same mistake when commenting upon another author's claim (hypothesis) that the poor verbal IQ of children with reading disabilities is related to the sort of physiological disorder specified by Luria. "However because it is based on Luria's observations, the hypothesis is extremely powerful in terms of specifying brain-behaviour relationships" (p. 253). What is a weakness in psychological theorizing has become, for Cummins and Das, a "strength."

Bruner (1976) has also declared support for his favourite discipline. He argues that, to explain behaviour, we must understand "the cognitive structures in terms of which the world is organized by the participants and, indeed, how language maps into those structures" (p. 1589). To do so he must deal with "intentions" and, to acquit "intentions" of the charge of inferential circular explanation, he must distinguish between "explanation by cause and description by intention" (p. 1590). As an example of the former, he offers the sentence "I am going to be sick": of the latter, "I am going to take a walk." Since the latter sentence implies that I am a controlling agent, failure to carry out my intention is interpreted as lying. Since the first sentence explicitly makes a prediction about future behaviour on the basis of antecedent sensations, the non-appearance of vomiting and sickness is regarded merely as a mistake.

However, even such a simple example presents problems. In the "lying" cases, Bruner does admit the possibility that the individual might adduce self-exonerating circumstances to explain away his behaviour, a tactic more frequently used than he cares to admit. Furthermore, the non-appearance of sickness might be regarded not as a mistake but as a trick or evidence of fearfulness. Again, the "lying" may have antecedents, i.e., the child may come from a broken home in which lying has been reinforced. And finally, if "intention" is used as part of an explanation—and it often makes sense to do so—the explanation can never become a Science 1 explanation unless "intention" can be measured in some reliable and valid way.

Bruner makes two further claims. The first is that the distinction between intentional or caused behaviour "is made all the time in all languages, all cultures, and is irresistible" (ibid.). The second is that, if causal explanations are to make any sense, they must be accompanied by the idea of "intention," present or absent. "It would be a vain enterprise to explain or even to discuss the causes of any human behaviour without taking into account whether or not intention had been attributed" (ibid.).

Against the first point, it might be argued that, in societal or legal practice, the distinction is often blurred or confused and is the source of endless argument because it has political overtones, i.e., does a welfare recipient not go out to work because he cannot be bothered (lack of intention) or because there is no work available (cause)? The same point has been made in the case of murder. The cogency of the second argument is a function of the extent to which the individual is willing to participate in Bandura's (1974) "infinite regression of causes" (p. 867). For example, Bandura (1973) defines aggression as "behaviour that results in personal injury and in destruction of property" (p. 5), making it clear that definition excludes socially-sanctioned injury such as dental repairs, and includes attempted aggression which fails. It might be argued that the definition could be reworded so that it incorporated these exemptions, and some ordinary behaviour in the Brunerian sense. That is, aggressive behaviour resulting in damage would have to be "intentional." For example, a person may accidentally stumble backwards and break the toe of a bystander. This is damage, but not in Bandura's sense. Again the dentist does not intend to be hurtful, and the unsuccessful assailant does so intend. Bandura is well aware of the notion of "injurious intent" (ibid.) which appears as the "intentionality criterion" in his earlier book with Walters (Bandura and Walters, 1963, p. 113). There it was criticized as having no explanatory value because of its inferential basis (p. 112), and was replaced by a "high magnitude" theory which proposed that aggressive responses are caused by the fact that a child, who learned to exhibit any responses with a high degree of intensity, is suddenly frustrated (pp. 116-117). This "high magnitude" theory is clearly unsatisfactory; a person who breaks another person's toe accidentally is not guilty of aggression, and to explain that person's behaviour in terms of a frustrated and aggressive childhood would be to go far back in the causal chain. Implausibly far.

The dilemma for a cognitive psychologist like Bruner (1976) is that, unlike behaviourists who ignore "intentionality" or reduce it to stimulus and response terms, he had always used the word while claiming to be a scientist (Bruner, 1970a, p. 51). He has made a brave case for employing "intentionality" to explain human behaviour (Bruner, 1975, pp. 34-35), but it is not part of the science game he pretends to practise, unless Dennett's (1978) unusual argument is accepted.

Bruner is also very much concerned about the applied value of psychology, but his position is marred by errors of a conceptual and chronological sort. A first error is his uncertainty about what is meant by the word "applied." Has psychology, he says, "affected issues of public concern on which it could reasonably be expected to have a bearing, say economics?" (1976, p. 1589). Implicit here is the erroneous assumption that contemporary economics has been successful in understanding and changing economic affairs (Gonick, 1976, p. 1) or even trying to solve real economic problems (Bose, 1975, p. 11). Moreover, psychologists have shied away from assessing the influence on people of the contemporary economic recession with its unacceptably high levels of inflation and unemployment, variables that influence people markedly.

Again, Bruner argues that psychology has been useless because of its early and continuing commitment to the "reductionistic" and "antimentalistic" approaches characteristic of the nineteenth century natural sciences. Now, he continues, "striking progress" is being made with cognitive psychology. "Developmental psychology . . . is moving nicely, thanks in large part to the impetus given by Piaget and Vygotsky" (p. 1589). There are at least two problems here. (a) All accounts of people (outside of existentialism) are reductionistic, Bruner's cognitive structures being an obvious example. (b) All early functional psychologists (Thorndike), associationists (Pavlov, Watson), Gestalt psychologists (Kohler) and ability psychologists (Binet, Burt, Terman) regarded themselves as natural scientists, although some were "mentalistic," others not. (c) At the moment the only useful psychology in any domain is the "anti-mentalistic" behaviour modification sort. Even in the latter case, its applied value has been restricted to people with limited degrees of freedom (seniles, mental retardates, children).

Bruner's own cognitive structures appear to describe very well the intellectual activity of scientists and technologists (Scribner and Cole, 1973), but their use-value in education has never been demonstrated and his claim that they have an impact "within and beyond psychology" (Bruner, 1976, p. 1589) is based on his own study of "the role of intention in early language acquisition, of intention as exhibited by the child and as perceived by the mother" (ibid.).

Presumably, psychologists can go on for more years pretending that this sort of study contributes both to a scientific psychology and to some other discipline. Returning to a study of the child's relations with his mother is a fairly harmless business if only because it will take some time, especially in a longitudinal study, to evaluate the long-term effects of this encounter between child and original model. The prospects look dismal because other models will appear (Skolnick, 1978). Another, more cynical point to be considered is that possibly the larger political and economic system has a strong interest in psychologists and their pretensions to the status of scientists because of their concentration on the great intellectual strides made in the much-heralded "magic years" of childhood. Bruner's talk of "the staggering rate at which the preschool child acquires skills, expectancies, and notions about the world and about people . . ." (Bruner, 1975, pp. 31-32) is "dead" (Smith and James, 1975, p. 228), but then so is Bruner's psychological science with its pretensions to marvellous discoveries. In which case, nobody wins: questions are asked about the value of studying such a soft science and teachers become the cause of the decline in educational attainment. Both groups, paid from public funds, are easy targets for criticism during a recession.

Church (1976), another champion of psychology as a science, offers an interdisciplinary approach in which bits of dubious psychology are mixed with economic homilies. Indeed, much of Church's work consists of statements of values and hopes pitched at the usual high level of abstraction preferred by social intellectuals with future scenarios. He—and everybody else—wants " . . . our own children to be loving, bright, well-informed, imaginative, articulate, humorous, generous, trustful, compassionate, serious, brave, and capable of sensuality" (p. 144) and, although he believes we can rear such children, he still hopes to design "new social institutions" that will help us to reach such a target. Just how these institutions will arise is not dwelt upon, a useful tactic since the current institutions of society (prisons, mental hospitals, schools and so on) do not produce people with many prosocial characteristics and there is no obvious way of getting rid of these institutions.

Church's next belief is that people, "as a matter of fundamental right," should have a decent share of the necessities of life (p. 145) which include food, clothing and shelter, "a ration of free energy" and free mass transportation and access to TV. Another necessity, not prefixed by the adjective "free," is a "full range of health services." Church does not explain why these are not "fundamental rights" at the moment, nor does he state how they can ever be realized in the future, especially when there are strong political and economic forces designed to keep things more or less as they are. This criticism applies to Church's other values and hopes. He wants a better distribution of wealth because, as he so rightly says, "there is no reason whatsoever that people should have to live in want and misery in the midst of plenty" (p. 147). "My solution . . . is to oblige (the giant corporations) to offer only goods of superior quality" (p. 247). Once the giants have obeyed his admonition, the unemployed will increase drastically, but they can "escape boredom by becoming artists, composers, poets, playwrights, actors and actresses, scholars . . ." (ibid.).

This is a dream, pleasant but unrealistic like those of Sperry and Bandura. Psychologists cannot change the present social order, the dangerous and unpleasant features of which are a consequence of powerful economic forces largely controlling the media and political system and limiting the values and understanding of the great majority of people. One of the forces is the vast increase in public spending which has been captured by the military or channelled into the building of roads for automobiles rather than into the less profitable task of clearing slums and building new houses for poor people (Baran and Sweezy, 1966, p. 295). Another factor causing both inflation and unemployment is the growth of multinational monopolies which fix prices so that, regardless of demand, they can set the profit levels which are their target. They can also create unemployment by shifting capital, plant, technology and technicians to areas of the world where workers, easily trained in minimal skills, are glad to accept relatively low rates of pay. Third, a significant jump in international oil prices has fuelled inflation and increased the price of gasoline, plastics, fertilizers and food, most of which are required daily by almost everybody (Gonick, 1976, p. 4). This situation is much worse in countries like the United States which use a vast amount of energy without having the manufacturing capacity to avoid a huge balance of payments deficit in the contemporary competitive world.

Enough has been said to indicate that, in the forseeable future, most people are going to have to learn to live with increasing amounts of inflation and unemployment, a decreasing standard of living and an increasing amount of crime. The only hope for psychologists working within the status quo is to get people to accept this state of affairs—a difficult task because most of the younger and middle-aged people in the population have known only relatively good times since 1941, and material progress is a dominant element in received opinion. Some psychologists are clearly aware of the problem. For example, Albee, a clinician, is quoted as saying: "I am not against psychotherapy, but we really ought to be spending our efforts in clinical psychology discovering the causes of the enormous amounts of distress in our society, and doing something about them" (in Galvin, 1977, p. E7). But Albee, like the rest, is vague about how to go about finding the sources and amount of "distress," perhaps because he could do nothing about them anyway. Unemployment and subemployment are obvious examples which, in contemporary society, not even politicians can attempt to reduce.

Platt (1973) has tried to plan a better social order by using the Skinnerian formula. For example, he treats social problems as "traps," unpleasant or lethal relationships among people from which there is no apparent exit. Moreover, he is more willing than Bandura to realize that some traps are "nested," i.e., promoted and reinforced by agencies, particularly the mass media, in the cultural milieu. Despite this, he assumes that these agencies can be offset by hypothesized community models of such significance that they can remove undesirable social behaviour by changing the direction of the reinforcers and by the establishment of a "superordinate authority" to allocate resources (p. 25). At the concrete level, he admits that the power of such an authority is limited to the setting of the amount of game or fish to be taken in a season. In larger matters—say the supply of natural gas or gasoline—Platt becomes cheerily abstract: the "superordinate authority" has the power " . . . to mediate conflicts, and to redirect reinforcement patterns to more rewarding long-range goals" (p. 25). This is at striking odds with the facts of industrial life in the United States where the various regulating agencies are manipulated by the corporations they are supposed to control. Quite harmless people have documented this point (Newfield and Greenfield, 1972, pp. 103-110).

The fact that they are not psychologists is important: if Platt is going to extrapolate from lab findings to provide remedies for the problems of the larger world outside, then he must know something about the dimensions of that world, particularly the fact that there already exist "superordinate authorities" in the form of large multinational corporations with profit-making goals which are almost completely at odds with the society of the future envisaged by Platt and Skinner. Indeed the "authorities" of the solid world often force a government, to its long-term disadvantage, to accept the conditions in which they will operate. Examples include the willingness of the seven large oil companies to keep the price of oil steady when supply was running ahead of demand in early 1975 (Sampson, 1976, pp. 359-360); the power of the automobile companies to block a 1976 amendment to the

1970 U.S. Clear Air Act (Asbell, 1976, p. 41); the extraction of financial concessions from governments (Mintz and Cohen, 1971, p. 31; Pratt, 1976, p. 7); and the ease with which multinational corporations can create national political havoc by moving investment and plant to low-wage countries (Ferrante, 1977). Likewise, the costs of any infrastructure (roads, airfields, city maintenance, and supplies of energy and water) used by private companies are often paid for by public funds, thereby diverting capital from projects that cater to human needs such as subsidized housing, public health, transportation, health and so on (Gorz, 1968, p. 87). The alternative plan of asking the corporations to provide their own infrastructures and diverting the capital saved to social ends is countered by blackmail in the form of threat to create unemployment by moving to another part of the globe where the "investment climate" is more favorable.

These powerful "superordinate authorities" and their representatives in the mass media can outmanoeuvre people and minor socializing agencies like the school partly by controlling the flow of information, advice and interpretation so that quasi-democracies exist in which "the powerful seek to rule without showing their powerfulness" (Mills, 1956, p. 317) partly by drawing attention away from serious social problems and focussing it on trivia like major team sports, and partly by sanctioning the use of legal and paramilitary power to prevent concerted action by dissidents (Alexander, 1976; Hoggart and Golden, 1971). In this way, they present the priorities of the present social system as given and normal, without major realistic alternatives, and they have been doing this for such a long time that people simply learn to cope within the existing framework. This is as true of Canadian farmers (Robertson, 1973) as of their Russian counterparts (Kaiser, 1976), although the kind of coping is different in the two groups.

The representatives of the larger social forces control people by means of the messages flowing to them, not by reinforcers administered in the Skinnerian fashion. People cope not because they are reinforced for doing so but because they are aware of the fact that they have no alternatives. This absence of any reference to the human situation characterizes Skinner's (1966) own embryonic ideas for improving society. He argues that man's contemporary difficulties are caused by the persistence of former reinforcers which once had survival value but which are now lethal. We eat too much, fight too much, and produce too many children, (1966, pp. 99-100). He suggests a variety of solutions to this problem, the most obvious of which is expressed in the following way. "Reinforcers can be made contingent on productive behaviour to which they were not originally related" (p. 164). But made contingent by whom and for what sort of productive behaviour? He does not say, merely asserting that "We must look instead at the conditions under which people govern, give help, teach and arrange incentive systems in particular ways. . . . Will a culture evolve in which no individual will be able to accumulate vast power and use it for stop his own aggrandizement in various ways which are harmful to others?" (pp. 226-227). Skinner thinks so. "Mankind has slowly but erratically created environments in which people behave more effectively . . ." (p. 227).

There are three reasons why this argument verges on the bizarre. "Mankind" should be replaced by "high technology developed by people so that the products increase company profits." Again, the human race has "created environments" deliberately and with purpose, not "erratically." Galton (1882, p. 197) made this point and clarified the term "effectively." Galton argues confidently that the "whole of the living world moves steadily and continuously towards the evolution of races that are progressively more and more adapted to their complicated mutual needs and to their external circumstances" (ibid.). Finally—and this is a criticism both of Skinner and of Galton—most people run for short-term material gains, a habit that sustains the economic system and is promoted by it. The few who are concerned about leaving a decent society and environment for future generations have no authority.

Some psychologists have agreed that the boundaries of the discipline must be extended in some way to include social influences. A gallant try at placing psychology in an historical context, a task made difficult because psychologists have managed to put an impressive distance between their discipline and political and social ideas—and for good reasons (Caute, 1978)—has been made by Albee (1977). Borrowing liberally from Weber's account of the "Protestant ethic," he argues that the success of capitalism required hard-working, thrifty people who could control their hedonistic impulses, especially of the powerful sexual sort. In short, the "outer directed" inhabitants of the older agrarian "shame cultures" had to become "inner directed" and directed by "guilt" in the form of a "tyrannical internalized conscience" (Albee, 1977, p. 152). Once these new people have been delivered by the Protestant faith, a problem arises: because of their asceticism and control of impulses and not, as is usually assumed, because of their relative poverty, they are unable to consume the output of a fantastically productive economic system. Indeed, Albee manages to transform economic conflict into psychological conflict by collapsing time in the following paragraph.

> But as production expanded beyond all reasonable bounds, and as the middle class spread far down the social order to include the great mass of wage earners, a paradoxical situation developed—the ascetic Protestant ethic was incompatible with the high level of consumption required to use up the flood of goods produced (p.158).

Nowadays, accordingly, industrial societies are inhabited by self-indulgent and sexually hedonistic people. "Increasingly, sex is becoming recreational rather than procreational" (p. 151). Albee believes that "there is a growing and pervasive sense of meaninglessness, nihilism and purposelessness" (p. 159) and that "fewer neurotics means more psychopaths" (p. 160). Poverty, unemployment, inflation and energy shortages are not on Albee's list; for him the source of the problems is self-indulgence.

The key to the weaknesses in Albee's paper is his replacement of economic conflict with psychological conflict and the errors and distortions this entails. Certainly one of the contradictions of capitalist societies, a point noticed before, is the inability of people to consume the goods produced, with resulting cycles of unemployment. This was caused by low wages, not by any asceticism (Hobsbawm, 1975, p. 218). As Marcus (1974) points out, dealing with Engels' 1844 *Condition of the Working Class in England*: the classical diagnosis of the culture of poverty . . . is its tendency to be impulse-ridden . . . in addition to drunkenness, Engels discusses the other classical components of this syndrome: impulsive and promiscuous sexuality, general improvidence, lack of foresight, inability to plan for the future, insufficient internalization of disciplines, regularities and normative controls and adaptive inflexibilties. (Marcus, 1974, pp. 109-110). If people can look forward only to the same dismal life they had experienced in the past, why should they be ascetic (Hoggart, 1961, p. 80)?

Another contradiction of capitalist society is also dealt with in unrealistic psychological terms by Albee. This economic conflict, the lack of a feed-through from profits into adequate wages, is explained as a product of the hypothetical spread of the "middle class" (and their asceticism) "to include the great mass of wage earners" (Albee, 1977, p. 154). This is palpably false even if the undefined term middle class is taken to include shopkeepers, the small bourgeoisie and farmers and even if the newer members of the "middle class" are declared to have risen by hard work from the "educated proletariat" (ibid.). This vague handling of the term "middle class" is characteristically American (Hodgson, 1976, pp. 479-483); the notion of an "educated proletariat" flies in the face of the poor quality of the public education that existed in nineteenth-century America (Hofstadter, 1966, pp. 300-301) and, as has been noted before, "the great mass of wage earners," usually two-thirds of the population (Hodgson, p. 481), have never been noted for thrift and asceticism. On the contrary, beyond the need "to make ends meet," these people enjoyed themselves in whatever way they could afford: by attending music halls and greyhound racing, by drinking a great deal of cheap liquor and by taking cheap excursions into the countryside (in Pyke, 1967, pp. 78-79). "Amidst all this ready expenditure of money on dress, or drink, or pleasure, there appears to be little that leaves any very permanent results in acquisition of other than temporary benefits. Such actual saving as we hear of is for the sunny rather than the rainy day" (p. 80). Even the relatively wealthy do not live an ascetic life (Albee, 1977, pp. 168-179). Indeed, during Victorian times there was a great deal of sexual activity, difficult to label as "repressed," in all classes (pp. 80-81; Marcus, 1966) which has become more openly talked and written about since 1945 (Lewis, 1978).

Consistent with the theme that Albee has been substituting psychological for economic concepts is the fact that, since he has freely assumed that almost everyone is in the "middle class," the many strikes and the advent of left-wing political parties in the nineteenth century are completely ignored. In this way he can also screen out the unconstitutional harrassments and para-military force with which these activities were put down in the United States (Alexander, 1976) and avoid the unseemly mention of politics and economics, although his psychotherapeutic confreres, Maslow and Rogers, have regularly posed as business consultants (Rogers, 1970, p. 125; Wilson, 1972, p. 182). Because he is unaware of Weber's critics (McCormack, 1969), Albee has reconstructed history into a series of events that are explicable in terms of a simple dimension of behaviour (asceticism—self-indulgence) within the professional domain of the psychologists. However, for this dispensation he has to pay the price of egregious historical and economic mistakes and of unsupported psychological speculations like "Fewer neurotics mean more psychopaths."

Such interdisciplinary essays carry little conviction nowadays partly because of the sheer volume of information to be scrutinized, and partly because there is no professional way in which such an interdisciplinary education can be acquired. This approach which assumes that psychology is an empirical study of the psychological dimension of social problems, an orientation which would force psychologists to understand the social and historical setting of behaviour and the variety of nonpsychological influences with which people have to cope, is utopian and dangerous. The location of psychology in a historical and social context would require consideration of topics like the destruction of mediaeval society and its replacement by a liberal technocratic one; the gradual development of monopoly capitalism, its use of advertising and automation, and its contribution to unemployment and a deteriorating environment and the history of psychology as a putative science caught up in these forces. Only Broadbent (1973) made a tentative (and interestingly unsuccessful) attempt to do this.

American psychologists rarely understood the student unrest of the 1960s and early 1970s (Travis, 1975, pp. 11-17) and those who did try tended to ignore the basic theme of the activitists, that university research and teaching were buttressing inequalities in Western societies (Miles, 1971). Protest movements—the American blacks in the South, the coalition against the Vietnam war and, later, the feminists—had made these inequalities more salient than ever before. Even social learning theorists ignored campus events although, rightly or wrongly, they were ready to berate Jensen for playing down the formative influence of a poor environment and milieu on IQ performance. In other words, professors had their dilemmas as well as students (Rubinstein, 1969). On the supposition that student protests were sociological or political phenomena (p. 134), psychological scientists continued on their chosen path of finding a basic theory of behaviour, or pluralistic theories for different domains. Piaget (1972) continued his work on logical cognitive structures and even the socially perceptive Bruner wisely left for Oxford in the early 1970s where he could safely carry on with his earlier work on coding. Significantly it was Broadbent (1973), a British psychologist, who replied directly to criticisms that empirical psychologists were supporting a social structure characterized by intolerable inequalities. However, as will be seen, even Broadbent, with the advantage of experiencing social democracy at work (at least in an embryonic way) lacked a sufficient acquaintance with social affairs to defend empirical psychology adequately.

Broadbent, an engineer turned psychologist, writes in the information-processing tradition:

> We have ... a position ... that a man is limited in his ability to process information; that this limit is a central one rather than one due to sensory or motor limitations; that as a result he selects only parts of his surroundings for response; and that this selection can take place through at least two different kinds of mechanisms (Broadbent, 1971b, p. 25).

The first mechanism, filtering, refers to the reduction of overload by the selection of items of information or even events with a common attribute for serial or simultaneous processing (Broadbent, 1973, pp. 174-178). The second mechanism, "pigeon-holing," refers to the way people combine information to achieve the most correct (and the fewest incorrect) decisions in any situation.

For example, if people are using an unreliable computer to help them detect a faint signal from another source, they will change or shift the criterion for recognizing that signal to correspond to their assessment of the probability with which the computer is functioning accurately. The report of a signal from a reliable computer is accepted, as is the non-report from a risky computer (p. 59). Again, more common words are easier to perceive than uncommon ones, as are misperceptions of the former (p. 27).

Such an active theory of perception and decision-making causes trouble for Broadbent who takes his science—and Hull—seriously and dislikes teleological notions like "purpose" (p. 40). His only alternative is to move words around in a way that signifies nothing, explains nothing. He opts for a postulated "fiat of will" (p. 26) which "is held inside the head," and is labelled a "command signal" or "intention." This is a set of "homunculi" going by different names and phrases. Equally problematic for Broadbent's theory (but not for him) is that it derived from the performance of unrepresentative subjects on unrepresentative tasks. His subjects, at least in the experiments listed in his 1973 book, are psychology undergraduates and their wives who make decisions about information that is unreliable or difficult to detect: listening over a noisy telephone line (p. 36); reading words on a poor carbon copy (p. 54); listening to faint signals from an unreliable computer (pp. 58-59); the detection of irregularly presented signals (p. 275) and so forth. In a representative and informative context like reading a more active approach to perception becomes feasible; on the basis of the meaning of past and present passages, hypotheses about what is about to be taken in are established and corroborated or changed.

The tasks and the samples, that is to say, are nicely chosen so that their performance is almost certain to support Broadbent's theory, but they are quite at odds with his previous idea about the greater probability that a practical rather than a "pure" psychologist would make a significant contribution to theoretical psychology.

> One reason for this is the sense of realism which is forced upon the applied man: he cannot choose specially favourable conditions for testing his theories, but must expose them to the full range of circumstances that may apply in his field (Broadbent, 1971b, pp. 17-18).

There is little point in criticizing Broadbent's theory partly because an earlier version has been handled roughly by Neisser (1967, pp. 208-210) and partly because getting to the pitch of Broadbent's claims requires an examination of his application of the theory to the political situation. Let us assume, then, that Broadbent is right; that the behaviour (perception and decision-making) of people must be functionally associated with their sense of the limited capacity and reliability of the brain and central nervous system so that critical levels for the acceptance of information can be adjusted (the criterion shifted) and the best possible outcomes assured after the information is stored and retrieved.

This is plausible enough. What is implausible—and what separates him from an American like Neisser—is his contention that this theory has a political counterpart in the existence of "Shadow Cabinets" whose members, in Opposition, provide extra information so that the Government can operate more efficiently. In fact it is the business of the Opposition to hammer and denigrate the policies of the the Government, and of the Government to fight back on each count, leaving the decisions of any representative assembly to be made by the members of the backroom committees helped by appropriate civil servants. Broadbent's associated notion that the political correlate of active perception is some form of totalitarian government is too ludicrous to warrant discussion. The exponents of such an approach to perception like Gregory (1974) and Neisser would regard this political insinuation as unwarranted, not to say insulting.

Broadbent also believes that his idea of a "command signal" is compatible with "freedom." The signal represents an "internal control" over behaviour which can be interfered with by societies that do not emphasize it much either for political or economic ends (1973, pp. 110-111). "Freedom," according to Broadbent, can be achieved only if people know the "biases" in their culture and limitations of their nervous systems. It is "one purpose of psychology to reveal these forces to us" (p. 111). At the personal level he discusses the advantages and disadvantages of the serial (successive or filtering) as against the holistic (simultaneous) strategies of processing information (p. 115). At the cultural level, Broadbent believes that, just as the serialist (scientific) mode of thought was applied to the external world in the seventeenth century, the domain of "consciousness" being left to "holism,"

> so now we are going to control ourselves more fully. This will mean treating our own modes of thought as being capable of alterations, just as our forefathers began to treat the English landscape, draining swamps, changing methods of cultivation . . . . The twentieth century shift will also mean an increased awareness of other people's state of mind as being different from our own. Given massive economic interdependence, our own intentions can only be translated into action in the light of other people's intentions and needs, and we cannot judge those by examining our own consciousness (p. 118).

This "freedom" can be arrived at only under certain conditions: people are aware of other "hypotheses and points of view" (p. 119); people appeal to external criteria to guide them in uncertainty; communications across cultural and personal barriers are based on external, observable events, and institutions are established which recognize a plurality of moral and religious points of view (p. 120).

This is the sort of light-fingered thinking Broadbent would never engage in while doing his psychological science. Consider just a few of the muddles. Freedom for any person in any culture usually means the restriction of someone else's freedom (Galbraith, 1980). It does not mean, outside of paradise, paying attention to somebody else's point of view. Second, this contention has an historical basis. The scientific approach to nature was linked to a corresponding empirical and associationistic approach to knowledge which gave way to Adam Smith, the Manchester School of economics and the rampant egoism of the nineteenth century "captains of industry" (Carey, 1979). Finally, our own modes of thinking can be altered but not by psychologists like Broadbent and other intellectuals. In this respect the media, totally ignored by Broadbent, are far more effective in shaping and altering attitudes. In fact, it is possible that Broadbent is paying more attention to the thoughts of intellectuals than to the appetites and customs of ordinary people.

Again, he relates his results from the signal-detection experiments to what he considers to be the "unemotional and technical" approach to government in Britain by what he pleases to call "Socialists" for some years after 1945. The "professionalism" of the view that "Socialism is about the division of wealth" is preferred to the position he attributes to Chomsky, who has certain anarchistic leanings (Chomsky, 1968), that "Socialism is about the liberation of the creative impulse"—an idea that smacks of an emotionalism detested by Broadbent.

Difficulties arise from this transfer of findings from one domain to a quite different one. First, the detection of a faint signal has no connection with the more emotional and value-laden business of governing a country. The "Socialists" with their cool professionalism generated heated conflict inside the party, a point already noted. The current divisive policies of the Thatcher government, based on an equally technical approach to the control of the money supply, has produced the same effect and is considered by its supporters as "liberationist" as Chomsky's "Socialism."

Again, Broadbent's transfer of procedure raises the problem of who is winning in the political domain after the fashion of the signal detector using the evidence of his own senses and unreliable information from the computer. It is obvious that no comparison is possible, although there is an answer in the social sphere: the winners, especially in contemporary societies of almost any kind, are those—a small percentage—who are rich, or at least the moderately affluent. Broadbent should know that cleaving to the strategy for making the best decisions in signal detection bears no relation of any kind to social and economic justice, a moral consideration (Jenkins, 1980, p. 4).

Broadbent dislikes the use of emotionally loaded words in social matters: he notes their disruptive impact without mentioning the fact that they are often necessary for calling attention to some desirable goal such as reducing unemployment, to increasing welfare benefits and to the new conception of the human condition that they entail. However that may be, he concludes, after a series of investigations into the effect of emotionally loaded words on perceptions of the word and the next word, that aroused people develop "funnel vision"; they collect information predominantly from one region of the environment which happens to be dominant, and neglect other sources which are also available.

There are two questions to be asked here. First, does "funnel vision" come before emotion or vice versa? The latter may be the case: there is a good probability that the accumulation of past beliefs, activated on an appropriate cue, leads to some emotional state and, in turn, to "funnel vision." For example, few Americans bothered very much about the presence of a U.S.S.R. puppet in Afghanistan—in fact almost no one knew about this state of affairs—until his incompetence forced the Russians to invade that country to pacify it. Then fears of spreading Russian imperialism began to be expressed. Furthermore, Broadbent assumes that the scientific attitude is "impersonal," not emotional, as is evident in their reporting of research. There is, however, another approach: scientists are just as emotional about their ideas as other investigators; they are cowed and brought to heel only by the intractability of the data with which they deal (Medawar, 1964). Social scientists are different because the data which they discuss, analyze, and ignore, can be altered and moulded to suit them (McGuire, 1973). Accordingly, it is unrealistic for Broadbent (1973) to take the position that ordinary people's decisions on social affairs will resemble those of the students working with an unreliable computer. Specifically, he believes that

> you will be more swayed by a pronouncement from a man who rarely takes sides than by the opinion of the sort of over-exposed letter-signer who is always protesting about something. Ingleby's results on the relationship between a computer and a human listener apply roughly to your judgements in social situations. It is entirely reasonable that this should be so: life is short, information scarce and unreliable, and our judgement and experience faulty. By combining evidence and biasing our decisions in this way, we can attain a high rate of success and partially overcome our own limitations (p. 61).

This excursion from the lab to society is such a disaster that it is difficult to select from the range of targets offered. What is meant, for example, by "taking sides" or a "high rate of success"? In point of the former term, most informed people "take sides"—it might have gone hard with Broadbent if Churchill had not replaced a fence-sitter like Chamberlain in 1940 (Soames, 1979, p. 286)—but they tend to take different sides because making decisions about social affairs, unlike detecting faint signals, involves value judgements. This means that, in the social scene, a "high rate of success" should be discarded in favour of notions like "value based emphasis" or "winning elections." Thus Thatcher won the 1979 British election because—as she saw it—of her faith that reducing inflation and increasing "freedom" were far more important (and incompatible) targets than the consensus politics ("Socialism") approved of by Broadbent. Policies of cutting taxes and restricting the money supply have had social and industrial consequences such as strikes, an increase in unemployment because of the inflated value of the currency, and a very rough time ahead for the poor, none of which would have been condoned by Broadbent. Yet they are the result of technical decisions based on value judgements that are formally similar to those employed by the "Socialists" after 1945. Only the substance of policies and judgements differ and these are not at issue in the drawing of comparisons between signal detection and the governing of a country.

Of course, Broadbent's primary claim is that society would benefit from the use of scientific methods. In a paper written in 1967 and published in 1973, he complains about the small per capita number of British psychologists as compared to that in the United States (Broadbent, 1973, p. 164) and points out that this is an unsatisfactory state of affairs because "we (psychologists) have acquired techniques for the study of human beings which will show a large return for further investment in the subject" (p. 186). He does not specify the recipient of this "return," although he dislikes people who question "the traditional approach of experimental psychology" (1971b, p. 7). He believes that if the facts were unearthed by empirical, preferably experimental , study, then people would not run to extreme views such as that psychology is "part of a capitalist plot designed to prevent students from asking searching questions, not merely about the nature of their own disciplines, but about the roots of power in the society in which they find themselves" (p. 8).

Although Ingleby (1974), author of the man-computer study, would use this last point to conclude that scientific methods cannot be used to study people and that those who carry out these procedures are trying to maintain the status quo (Ingleby, 1974, p. 317), it is possible to impale Broadbent on this point without making one with Reich or Laing who assume gratuitously that this maintenance of the status quo is deliberate. Rather, the general strategy for criticizing Broadbent, apart from the usual complaints about the unrepresentativeness of subjects and tasks studied, is to take seriously his own stance: the test of intellectual excellence of a psychological theory, as well as its moral justification, lies in its application to concrete practical situations" (Broadbent, 1971b, p. 7). One tactic is to point out that the eight to ten decades of experimental psychology have influenced societies and their fates not at all. Another is to gather evidence, by a wide variety of means, to criticize established ideas which are usually of service to those who are comfortable and relatively affluent. For example, contemporary budgets are touted as "realistic" which increase unemployment, reduce the money supply and, in the nature of things, do nothing at all about inflation which, at least in the short term, is beyond monetary control. Empirical psychologists should ask, "realistic for whom"? and then provide evidence instead of shouting obsolete war-cries in a jargon few understand. Finally, it must be understood that every society has its ruling authorities who will use any ideas to retain power to the extent that they can. In the U.S.S.R., for example, the Vygotsky-Luria thesis that thinking is closely related to speaking must have been quite acceptable to members of the Politburo, although the authors thought they were establishing a psychological science. The critical question is whether the authors deliberately set out to create a science with an eye on the political considerations and, on this count, American psychologists must be condemned.

There are enormous difficulties in translating lab-based findings to the unstable social events, even in industrial societies. Broadbent's professional career reached its peak in the 1950s and 1960s when (British) consensus ideals prevailed and the policies of different political parties were much the same (Blackburn and Cockburn, 1967; Thompson, 1960; Williams, 1968). Since these decades, the planet has become an unfriendlier place in which to live. Wars, strikes, guerrilla activities and small-scale revolutions are almost commonplace and a lack of mutual understanding at the international level is more salient than ever before. There is no evidence that psychologists have been able to mitigate these conditions because, like Broadbent (1973, p. 82), they still insist that the proper procedure is to establish or validate stable laws in a lab setting and possibly, like him, look for some social significance in these laws. His belief is pretentious in that, because of alleged parallels between the early seventeenth and late twentieth centuries—doubts about authority, leading to a shift in power from one group to another, and an acceptance of the idea that established scientific bodies should extend explorations of the physical world (Medawar, 1969, p. 18)—it is now appropriate to explore consciousness. Chronological parallels of this sort do not attract historians, and not even Broadbent's psychology is a science.

8 / ADMITTING DEFEAT

One way of extricating oneself from commitment to an erroneous position is to admit that a mistake has been made, to discover the source of that error and to formulate a more appropriate stance for the future. What, then, went wrong with the attempt to find reliable performance laws comparable to the successful physical laws of conventional science? Five reasons will be adduced to explain this failure; there are others (Gergen, 1973) but the accompanying five are considered to be the most salient.

A. "Dead Mechanism" and Animate Objects

Far from being inanimate objects, predictable and controllable, people are sometimes actively seeking after information and making value judgments and sometimes creatures of habit. No scientific theory of experience can even begin to capture this state of affairs without unproductive squabbling. Concerning Milgram's (1974) studies of obedience to authority, for example, it has been argued by Mixon (1974) that the overt meaning of the experiment was controlled by Milgram's deceitful instructions which appear to have had the same effect as Pavlov's apparatus on his dogs (Osgood, 1953, p. 405). Again, although cognitive psychologists never accept the behaviourists' position that the organism is a passive respondent to the stimulus, it has been argued by Argyris (1975) that their common use of the experimental method drives them into the same position of an uni-directional approach to causality and, by implication, into accepting the responses of the organism as relatively restricted. "In fact, the very capacities to behave in certain ways may be created or abrogated by the laboratory situation" (Harre and Secord, 1972, p. 48).

The fact is, however, that in everyday life people can be manipulated, sometimes into confessing that they have committed a criminal act of which they are innocent (Hilton and Shirley, 1980, p. 13), but in ways and with results quite different from those in the natural sciences. There are inducements and threats on the one hand, and hesitation, indecision, compliance

111

and successful resistance (as in Milgram's work) on the other. In Communist societies, the policies of established authorities are inculcated to a much greater degree than the information and commercials in the West but dissenting activities appear in the former societies. Human performance in certain domains can be predicted but with nothing like the certainty and consistency of objects in the natural sciences.

B. Sampling

There are at least two salient problems in this area: often subjects are eliminated from the middle range of a distribution of scores so that positive results can be obtained from the use of the resulting dichotomy, and most authors test available subjects and samples of subjects, university students and infra-human organisms especially, rather than more representative ones which are awkward to come by. For example, Bronfenbrenner (1970), using findings from tests administered to more than 150 twelve-year-olds (six classrooms in three different schools) in the U.S.S.R., England, West Germany and the U.S.A., wrote a book in which he blamed heavy TV viewing and membership in peer groups as the source of the greater aggression exhibited by American youngsters than their U.S.S.R. counterparts. No information is provided about where Bronfenbrenner found these 150 children in any of the countries. This is a serious defect in the study because in all the countries mentioned, and especially in the U.S.S.R. (Szamuely, 1969, pp. 54-55), pupils differ markedly in academic performance among schools in any one region.

More specific sampling problems are listed in White and Duker's (1973) scrutiny of 207 random samples of developmental studies in which they uncovered some serious yet simple psychometric errors. First, whereas information about accessible variables was always given (number of children, sex ratios and grade-level), only a small percentage of studies mentioned variables of greater theoretical and practical interest: family income (two percent); parental occupations (six percent), parental education (two percent); neighborhood (six percent); dialect spoken (zero percent) and ethnicity (two percent). Again, whereas social class was reported in 31 per cent of studies, only two per cent of them reported any measure of it (p. 701). The last omission is particularly unfortunate since even the most often used and available definition of class categories in the United States is palpably unacceptable (Hodgson, 1976, p. 480).

Second, almost 62 per cent of the samples consisted of children of the better-educated classes (professional and managerial) whereas only 18 per cent were drawn from areas inhabited by the working classes and the poor. Probably only 10 per cent of the population are in the former category—35 per cent if we want to include the "economic middle-class" listed by Heilbroner (1976, p. 39)—so that, at best, most studies deal with the children of only 16 per cent of the total population. As in most studies of personality, very little is heard about working-class parents and children, partly because of their inaccessibility and resistance to tests and partly because most researchers are more at home with well-educated people and their off-spring, the last point being supported by Hollingshead and Redlich (1958, p. 344) in the area of psychiatric practice. Understandably, if the sample is unrepresentative, authors would be unwilling to report simple descriptive statistics like the mean and standard deviation of scores on the standardized tests administered.

Third, the percentage of studies reporting information about the sampling of schools is disconcertingly small. Specifically the size of the total pool from which the sample was drawn was noted in only 14 per cent of studies; how school or schools were selected (four percent); how the class or classes were selected (15 per cent) and, the easiest information to get hold of, how the individual was selected (40 per cent). Complete information of these sorts was available in only 61 of the 207 papers studied. White and Duker most aptly quote Schultz (1969) to the effect that "We cannot continue to base some 80 per cent of our human subject data on college students and still call our work a science of human behaviour" (p. 224). This is also true of developmental studies in which the most able students, the ones that respond readily to experimental treatments, are tested.

It is a sad comment on the state of professional opinion that the only people who take sampling seriously, the commercial makers of standardized aptitude and attainment tests, are suffering undeserved criticism while more careless authors like Bronfenbrenner, using tests and subjects about which no quantitative information is provided, are left unscathed. One can assume only that psychologists will go to any length to treat, tacitly, any accessible sample of subjects as representative in order to garner the precious data they need.

C. Cause and Effect

It is often difficult to tell, regardless of the scientific method used, which variable is the cause and which the effect, and whether the conventional attribution of cause and effect is acceptable. Developmental psychologists have traditionally looked at parent-child relations in terms of the effects of the mother's personality and behaviour on the child. Indeed, in the context of contemporary dissatisfaction with the behaviour of the young, there is much advice abroad about proper parenting. "Most child-care advice assumes that if the parents administer the proper prescriptions, the child will develop as planned" (Skolnick, 1978, p. 45). And, by implication, if the child develops poorly, the parents (usually the mother) are to blame (p. 58). In fact, the relationship established between the effects of parents on children can easily be reversed. Bell (1968), Chess (1971) and Martin (1975) have emphasized the effects of children on parental behaviour. For example, the relationship between harsh parental discipline and children's aggressiveness may be caused as much by the presence of the latter as of the former variable as a cause. Again, children with biological problems may be battered by the mother because they have overtaxed her resources. Milowe and Lowrie (1964) found that the same children tended to be battered by different caretakers, a point which indicates that the children themselves have precipitated the abuse. More, Harper (1971) has drawn on human and animal research to illustrate the effect of the young in evoking sex-typed responses by parents. Finally, Mischel (1966) believes that the acquisition of sexual stereotypes is best described in terms of his variant of social-learning theory, i.e., little girls and boys learn sex-typed roles from sex-appropriate models. After reviewing several studies, Mischel concludes that "It seems very likely that in our culture girls receive more reward for dependency than boys" (p. 77). Unfortunately Mischel's studies are so designed that they prevent investigators from drawing the opposite conclusion, which is logically possible and has been verified by Hutt (1972, pp. 54-55, 102) that the biologically more docile girls and aggressive boys elicit sex-appropriate reinforcements from their parents. In the same way, children's performance is conventionally attributed to parental influence although they live in a context of other models, notably sportspeople, entertainers and peer group members, any one of which might exercise a more critical authority than parents; indeed they might direct the behaviour of parents and children. However, the parents, particularly the mother who is more accessible to researchers, are usually held responsible for the way the children comport themselves.

D. Shifty Facts

Evidence of the devotion of psychologists to fashionable ideas is particularly obvious in the changing data base of studies in sex differences and related functions during the decade between 1966 and 1976 when feminist movements became very salient. Since this sort of activism was good for business, mainly of a sartorial sort, and carried no obvious dangers to the established orders of society, it was given much publicity. Moreover, since it appeared to fall into the category of "impoverished potential" which touched off the wrath of social intellectuals at that time, there was a scramble to disavow former settled conceptions, to ignore the biochemical influence on behaviour and to report that sex differences were withering away. For example, before feminist activity became prominent, an early work was edited by Eleanor Maccoby (1966) whose summary of empirical studies pointed to many sex differences which she attributed to a biological and sociological interaction. "The biological underpinnings of the social demands for sex-typed behaviour set modal tendencies for cultural demands, and set limits to the range of variation of these demands from one cultural setting to another" (p. 50). These limits allowed for considerable variation both between cultures and within cultures, in what is considered "masculine" and "feminine," and for changes to take place in the "cultural demands" if these matched the "biological underpinnings" (ibid.).

This reasonable position was rejected in the summary of researches published in 1974 by Maccoby and Jacklin with the title *The Psychology of Sex Differences*. They conclude that only a few sex differences are "fairly well established" (1974, p. 351). (a) Girls have "greater verbal ability than boys," this superior performance appearing in all aspects of verbal work (including "creative writing") beginning at age 11. (b) Correspondingly boys "excel in visual-spatial ability" (ibid.), the difference beginning in childhood. (c) The excellence of boys in "mathematical ability" begins at the same time, but it is not so great as in spatial ability (pp. 350-351). (d) From about two years of age, boys are more aggressive, "both physically and verbally" (p. 352). Moreover, apart from sex differences in visuo-spatial ability and aggression, which are regarded as being biologically determined (p. 360), the remaining differences are learned, but the sex-typing is not blamed on the parents (pp. 339, 362). The inferences to be drawn are that women have only themselves to blame and/or they are unfairly discriminated against by men in positions of authority.

The later book presents several problems, acutely touched on by Block (1976). First, some important studies, almost all of a psycho-physiological sort, which would have altered or increased the number of Maccoby and Jacklin's conclusions, have been excluded or wrongly summarized (pp. 520-521). An important example is Hutt's *Males and Females* (1972) which is mentioned in the references but ignored in the text. This is a particularly serious omission because Hutt ties her findings to a biochemical thesis ignored by Maccoby and Jacklin who treat human beings as if they were fairies.

Second, Maccoby and Jacklin use a tabular or "box-scoring" method in which studies are simply tabluated by formal titles. This is a psychologically inappropriate procedure for a variety of reasons. (a) Topics which have some affinity are treated separately if they are labelled differently; an obvious example is the separation of studies in "reasoning" from those in "language" and "intelligence." (b) Accessible studies are lumped together without any reference to their quality; numbers of youngsters tested vary enormously across studies and, in most cases, information about their socio-economic status and their performance on a scholastic aptitude test is not given. (c) More than one-third of the comparisons between the sexes on performance are based on samples of less than 60 subjects (one fifth less than 40) and 75 per cent are of children 12 years old or younger (40 per cent are of preschoolers) (Block, 1976, p. 518).

Third, the "box-scoring" method which places findings in three categories—those favouring males, those favouring females and those with no significant differences—has resulted in an inappropriate analysis of the results which, since dealt with in detail by Block (pp. 519-530), need not detain us here. However, it is significant that the findings allegedly "overturned" since 1966 are those most feminists would reject: that females rather than males are significantly more "social" and "suggestible," have lower self-esteem, excel at rote-learning and simple repetitive tasks, are less "analytic" and more affected by heredity and lack of achievement motivation (Maccoby and Jacklin, pp. 349-351).

The erosion of the data base can also be attributed to the acceptance by Maccoby and Jacklin of the null hypothesis to mean a negative result, to their refusal to evaluate the quality of the research they summarize and to the authors' quixotic interpretation of their own summaries. An illustration of the last point is their unwillingness to believe that females are more "social" than males. This belief rests on the argument in a peculiar passage which begins by reporting that the 1966 summaries had

> indicated that women and girls showed more interest than boys in social activities and that their tastes in books and TV programmes were more oriented toward aggression, 'action,' and science than was true for boys; furthermore girls developed an interest in the opposite sex at an earlier age, and were more concerned about their personal appearance and attractiveness. To our knowledge nothing in the more recent research contradicts these conclusions. The danger simply is in overgeneralizing from them. Such findings do not warrant any conclusion that girls have a greater 'capacity' for social responsiveness. In fact, it is our opinion that the social judgment skills of men and boys have been seriously underrated (p. 214).

This slippery passage containing an implicit rejection of an accepted finding warrants attention. (a) Theoretically, findings do not imply "capacity" if a social-learning theory of behaviour is used, as it usually is at Stanford where Maccoby teaches. (b) The first part of the statement runs counter to Maccoby and Jacklin's contention that it is erroneous to claim that females are more social than males (pp. 349-350). (c) The second part of the statement is gratuitous speculation. (d) Various phrases are treated as synonymous without any argument or evidence being advanced that would make their imputed equivalence realistic. Thus we have "gentleness in interpersonal relations," "social responsiveness" and "social judgment." Conceptually, these terms are not synonymous and the meaning of even one term may be different in different settings.

Few will doubt that feminist movements are justifiably irritated at the treatment of women in many societies, including the U.S.S.R. (Kaiser, 1976, pp. 61-61). And this for two reasons: (a) the unwarranted exclusion of highly-qualified women from work for which they are particularly suited (law, medicine and theology are obvious examples) and (b) the downgrading and poor evaluation of work for which they are particularly suited by biological disposition—fine digital performance, attention to detail and interpersonal concerns that often culminate in a maturity rarely achieved by men. It is the latter point that dogs the social scientist: there are reliable differences between male and females in performances which can be reasonably related to biological disposition (Hutt, 1972), but female performances are judged to be so menial by dominant and articulate males that their sexual counterparts are roused to deny the very existence of the differences and to insinuate that women are deliberately funnelled into these menial tasks by bigoted males. To all appearances, a matter of fact has been transformed into one of values.

An associated problem is that most feminists and their male supporters are social intellectuals, quite unrepresentative of ordinary people and their restricted life-chances. To the former group the accurate, routine digital work, often done by women, is disgraceful and degrading. For example, Mitchell (1971) is enraged by the employment of women in a biscuit factory that was not automated. "The women stood in line simply packing different shaped biscuits into differently shaped boxes as they came along the conveyor belt" (p. 128). The foreman told Mitchell that men could not do the task because they could not keep their attention fixed on it. After listing one woman's remark to the effect that women were brought up to look demurely down and that this fitted them for packing biscuits, Mitchell asks, "Does women's social training fit them for monotonous work?"

Mitchell ignores certain facts. (a) Most people have to do "monotonous work" at some time of their lives, and many men spend their entire lives at it. In the biscuit factory, the men sweeping the floor are not mentioned by Mitchell as doing "monotonous work." More, what about barbers, painters, truck drivers, meter-readers, garbage-collectors and almost all the entire range of occupations done by ordinary people? In a heavily-automated society, these jobs must be the ones not worth automating and, hence, "monotonous." (b) Mitchell did not ask whether the women preferred the biscuit-packing to the alternatives (if any) available to them. It is, after all, a skill suited to their fine digital performance which men cannot match (Hutt, 1972, p. 97). Only a small number of people have the talent or opportunity to do "creative," let alone professional, work and it is significant that "creative" women disproportionately more often than men fall into the non-scientific category, as do the feminists themselves (writers, instructors in the social sciences, history and literature, or freelance journalists).

This is not to deny "equality of opportunity" to women, nor is it to deny the unjustifiable discrimination against them in the past (Okin, 1979). Rather it is to assert that the non-sexual behaviour of men and women—and particularly the areas of work for which they are specially fitted—may have a biochemical basis (Hutt, 1972, pp. 58-59, 95-96, 112-113). The notion advanced by Unger (1980) that sex differences are physiological whereas "gender differences" are learned is unrealistic (English, 1980) and hostile to Hutt's contention that, given equal access to education, women should perform much better than men in prestigious occupations like medicine and law for which they are uniquely equipped. If a social learning (environmental) viewpoint is adopted, women may, often do, make claims to an equality that denies biological reality and/or irritates the rest of the community in question. Probably there should be more female than male physicians, lawyers and perhaps computer programmers and official religious representatives, but the reverse should be true of mathematicians, physicists and politicians.

The point being made here is that when opinions and value judgments alter interpretations and findings in less than a decade and when iconoclastic thinking is prohibited in certain areas because of strongly-held beliefs, then there is little hope of developing a psychological science in the domain under study. Mission-oriented research confirms all discrimination against women, regardless of whether it is justifiable or not. Unquestioned obedience to authority refers to acquiescence to the fashionable ideas and sentiments held at the moment by social intellectuals whose discipline, because of that, can scarcely lay claim to being an empirical study, far less any kind of psychological science.

E. Theoretical Squabbling

The main reason why psychological investigations are not part of a conventional science is their lack of any common theoretical framework and, indeed, the probability that this state is unattainable. Newell (1973) deals with a paper concerning short-term memory in which, he argues, its authors provide "yet one more explanation." "Regardless of the exact merits of the case . . . it can be stated with some confidence that their article does not settle the issue . . . (their work) provides good evidence for the general propositions that psychological issues have difficulty even fading away" (p. 290).

Indeed, Park (1976) argues that people find many reasoning problems difficult in the sense that they cannot falsify solutions because they have no frame of reference or structure within which their answer can be observed to be wrong, i.e., does not fit the explanatory structure available. "Thus if we ask a chemist to explain the reactivity of the SH radical in cysteine, we *expect* him to reply in terms of bond-strengths, ion sizes, and so on" (pp. 107-108). In psychology, however, there is no agreed general structure within any domain and no possibility of eliminating the wrong answers as a main way of reaching the right answer. The standard tactic, much more heavily relied on by psychologists than by students in the more exact sciences, is to gather information in support of a theory and to eliminate, at least for a time, recalcitrant findings by "patching" the theory to fit standard and the anomalous findings. This is a reasonable approach if the original theory is useful and there are no plausible rivals available. However, after this patching has reached unwarranted lengths and the anomalous findings have been gathered into an acceptable new theory, the conventional theory is discarded. This is never an easy change, even in the physical sciences (Barber, 1961); in the social sciences it is almost impossible because the many dated theories are simply laid aside to be resurrected when the dust of the original destructive controversy has settled. Freudian ideas have been unearthed (Jacoby, 1975; Silverman 1976); Adler has been used by Dreikurs (1972) and Rank by Becker (1973). Simplified gestalt notions have informed the version of transactional analysis preferred by James and Jongeward (1976). A variant of idealism has reared its head (Weimer, 1974) and McDougall and Jung are allotted space in Hogan (1976).

F. In the Laboratory

As putative natural scientists psychologists understandably worked in a laboratory or other experimental setting. The problem arising from this defect is not that variables are controlled by external forces but that they are controlled by different forces and to a different degree. Youngsters can be trained to exhibit altruistic behaviour in an experimental setting, but this never transfers to everyday life in which people are usually reinforced to look to their own advantage. The equipotentiality premise, that behaviour studied in the laboratory is representative of other behaviours, is a form of special pleading by experimentalists whose status depends on the acceptance of their claim to be scientists. Not even Skinner accepts that premise any more.

If there are no stable causal laws, except possibly the Law of Effect which is in bad odour because of its association with hedonism and behaviourism, and no stable probabilistic ones, which are strongly disliked by experimentalists, what survival plans are available to psychologists who have to admit defeat as scientists?

9 / SURVIVAL PLANS

Since psychology is not a science in any sense of that term (Anderson, 1981), the academic value of its study of behaviour or psychological functions is questionable, especially in a time of recession, professional unemployment and a steady decline in birth rates. One solution is to treat the discipline not as a "science" but as a set of empirical studies of potential value to other disciplines like history. Such a study would provide psychologists with a glimpse of the social milieu which they have formerly avoided to their detriment. Admittedly there are no good precedents to follow, but a beginning can be made by considering versions of a "human science" which would irritate any conventional scientist.

A. The Human Science

Exponents of psychology as a human science, Harre and Secord (1972) in Britain and Giorgi (1970, pp. 194-195) in the United States, dislike the application of the methods of the natural sciences to human performance. They are forced to describe "human science" as some understanding of the total human experience or "experiential behaviour dialectics." Here the two groups part company. The British group describes these dialectics in terms of a list of variables; the presence of many "social selves" directing behaviours (p. 93) and the "open souls doctrine" which means that the "phenomena which people presume to report both *really* exist and *are relevant*" (p. 105), an idea that would have irritated Freud. Finally, they describe their own approach to people in a simpler and less specific way than Giorgi. "We should treat people, for scientific purposes, as *if they were human beings*, as we know and understand them in everyday life" (p. 87).

Although Giorgi (1970) admits that he has no precise definition of human nature (p. 201), nevertheless he knows what the "human sciences" are supposed to be studying. His list of terms include meaning, description, qualitative differences, the process of explicitation, investigating intentional relations, dealing with human phenomena in a human sense and in a human way, articulating the phenomena of consciousness and behaviour, within the context of a broadened conception of nature, and assuming the privileged position of the life-world, the primacy of relations and the presence of an involved scientist (p. 205).

Roughly similar to Harre and Secord and Giorgi is Buss's (1979) recent "hermeneutic dialectic science" which is "committed to arriving at valid intersubjective meanings and *thereby facilitating communication and enhancing greater understanding*" (Buss, 1979, p. 180). This "metascience" is said to be "based upon the values of the democratization of knowledge and human emancipation" (p. 190). Beneath these assertions lie three assumptions acceptable to Buss: that psychology should be concerned with the mutual interaction among cognitions, behaviour and conditions (p. 167); that "facts" about people are interpretations stemming from a theory laden with values (p. 16), and that the most "democratic" theories are the best, Dewey's educational theory being given favourable mention.

Although Harre and Secord do offer a method for understanding human performance, Buss is content with Feyerabend's (1975) argument that conventional scientific methodologies and findings are unacceptable because they are at odds with certain moral values like "a humanitarian attitude" and "liberty" defined as follows:

> The attempt to increase liberty, to lead a full and rewarding life, and the corresponding attempt to discover the secrets of nature and of man entails, therefore, the rejection of all universalist standards and of all rigid traditions. (Naturally, it also entails the rejection of a large part of contemporary science) (p. 20).

Moreover, since the conventional way of doing science supports "the established order of things," this order must be destroyed so that "human spontaneity may come to the fore and exercise its right of freely initiating action, of freely choosing what it thinks best" (p. 187). Feyerabend supports a variety of methodologies which will keep different theories in the air so that people can choose the one that suits them. Knowledge is

> an ever increasing ocean of mutually incompatible (and perhaps even incommensurable) alternatives, each single theory, each fairy-tale, each myth that is part of the collection forcing the others into greater articulation and all of them contributing via this process of competition, to the development of our consciousness (p. 30).

This anarchistic approach to knowledge is probably more applicable to psychology than to the natural sciences in which findings must be publicly verifiable by neutral authorities. In psychology, where "facts" like "He is aggressive" are often interpretations based on value-laden theories, a variety of these theories may appear and be chosen as valuable by different people for different purposes. That is, a basket of solutions and remedies which, although quite disparate conceptually, may be useful in a variety of different situations. Distinguished psychologists have made informative and non-trivial discoveries. Their mistake has been to push these ideas beyond the scope of their valid applicability (Rapoport, 1978/79, p. 660), and to promote the assumption that their "laws" resemble those of the natural sciences. A greater humility is in order.

B. Humble Solutions

First, it is important not to abandon conditional laws, especially in areas like psychophysiology. The brain is a physical system and the study of its psychological implications should be encouraged despite baffling psychological and philosophical problems entailed in the study of brain-behaviour relationships. This bafflement may be only temporary: one never knows what will be round the corner. Likewise, the successes of behaviour modification therapy should encourage people to contemplate the occasional value of Skinner's position for the diagnosis and alteration of behaviour. After all, Skinner's values look to be fairly "humanistic" (Krasner, 1978, p. 802).

Second, although the findings from correlational analyses and experiments in cognitive psychology are practically valueless, they are better than no findings at all. Trouble begins when findings are given a strong psychological interpretation which so disregards the power of environmental variables that negative results must be tampered with so that the psychologist can claim that something other than his discipline has gone wrong. Head Start, for example, was backed by Hunt's (1961) contention that "intellectual capacity" (p. 362) could be improved during the early years of childhood with an accompanying "substantially higher adult level of intellectual capacity" (p. 363). Since Head Start has failed to bring about this desired change, Hunt must now recite his old research, conclude that the Head Start programs were insufficiently "enriched" (Pines, 1979, p. 67), and that poor mothers could develop the "intellectual capacity" of their child if they started "right at the lying-in hospital" (p. 64).

Hunt's problem is well known (McGuire, 1973, p. 449): convinced of the rightness of his thesis and regardless of a variable like the anti-educational experience of the underprivileged child, he concludes that there must be something wrong with the experiments affecting the implementing of the psychology behind the thesis. Accordingly, he believes that Head Start programs must be improved: the mother must start the enrichment process from the first day of the child's life and carry on until some highly-educational day-care service takes over. No thought is given to the unrealistic nature of the suggestion, particularly to questions like how a poor mother is going to start the enriched program, who is going to fund the day-care centres and how will the encroaching anti-educational experience of the growing underprivileged child be fended off? Hunt maintains the central significance of his psychology by ignoring these considerations, although Smith and James (1975), noting the rise in criterion performance of an experimental group after a year and its sudden decline after two years to the level of a control group, conclude that:

The disadvantaged are those who have systematically lost out in the struggle for scarce resources; different patterns of socialization and different emphases in early development are in part a necessary adaptation to these harsh realities . . . . Preschool intervention alone makes no impact on these factors; once it is withdrawn they reassert themselves (p. 237).

Third, Canadian educational researchers should ignore psychology in favour of becoming specific with regard to the educational aims accepted by the authorities in question, to the educational programs likely to realize these aims, and to the measurement criteria regarded generally as appropriate. For example, far too much time has been spent on the American fad of discovering the earliest time when a concept can be learned by a child, despite the fact that this feat may bear only a negligible relationship to the total learning of the older pupil. Researchers and thinkers should strive to avoid the errors and contradictions embedded in easily-forgotten provincial documents, to ignore vacuous questions like "What is the optimum class size?" and to be enterprising enough to try out and advance new ideas which pay attention to pupils as not altogether man-machine systems. The new minicomputers will certainly alter significantly much professional training, but it is far too soon to announce that future teachers will be merely tenders of educational hardware because not all students will necessarily be any more keen to learn from hardware than from teachers. If past experience is a useful guide (Travis, 1979, p. 198), the failure of this updated electronic gadgetry to improve school performance is predictable.

Finally, the most general and humble solution must encompass work on "human science" as well as that dealing with human and probabilistic laws. It would be easy to dismiss "human science" for what it is, an untested (and probably untestable) moving of words around until they make people, especially its users, happy. The question rising early in the friendliest mind must point to its unrealistic nature as a series of propositions about people, now or in the foreseeable future. What does the word "human" mean embedded in phrases like "treating people as if they were human beings" and "dealing with human phenomena in a human sense and in a human way"? What of people living at or below the poverty line (Adams, 1971)? What about the treatment meted out to coalminers (Caudill, 1977), to prisoners (Abbott, 1980) and to those unfortunate enough to be locked up in mental hospitals (Rosenhan, 1973, pp. 254-257)? What of the many people whose skills are being automated out of existence? How would the "human scientists" deal with Bettelheim's (1961) contention that living in a metropolis resembles living in a concentration camp, or Jacoby's (1975) conclusion that "human relations" have yet to be realized for many people in contemporary existence?

However, this is brutal and unfair to human scientists because their natural science counterparts, who rarely use the word "human" except in an abstract way, have never even faced these questions. More to the point, some psychologists are enthusiastic about "human science" while the other psychologies command respect often because of their institutional support. A decent compromise would be to consider all psychologies as belief systems which might be informative and useful on certain occasions. In the realm of theory, no author should lay initial claim to a greater scientific status than others, but the belief system must be capable of being replicated by other competent researchers (Medawar, 1969) and there is no good reason why different theories as belief systems should not coexist in the repertoire of helping professions.

There are two additional advantages of seeing psychology as a set of beliefs. First, it is consistent with the idea that the model/helper, not so much the theory, is of value in the interpersonal therapeutic situation (Drummond, 1978) or the classroom. Second, for too long psychologists have prided themselves on their devotion to techniques and quantification, and anything that looks "scientific" to the unquestioning eye, despite the fact that they have produced nothing of consequence and are derided by natural scientists. It is time to restore this imbalance by encouraging psychologists to be widely-read, knowledgeable and literate students of humane and cultural studies. This is not to deny that there is some professional value in having a nodding acquaintance with techniques; rather it is to assert that substantial contributions to the understanding of people can be made without the student or researcher being bogged down in methodological and conceptual morasses (Koch, 1978, p. 638; MacRae, 1974, p. 84).

Finally, an acceptance of psychology as a set of belief systems instead of the aping of the natural science requires all psychologists to take a more benignly critical approach to the research of their colleagues. There is no room for Harre's and Secord's (1971, p. 78) castigation of the natural science approach as a "mechanical model," inappropriate to the study of human performance. Many psychologists like that model and its therapeutic value is without rival. Others may prefer Harre and Secord's "anthropological model" or Giorgi's "human science," and the disagreements about any aspect of the different theories should be between friends. Any suggestion that this may lead to chaos can be offset by pointing to the more inflamed chaos that currently exists, together with the cynicism, nicely expressed by McGuire (1973), about the value of psychology as a way of understanding people.

It may well be argued by Marxists like Bowles and Gintis (1976) that this thesis about the liberal consensus is not new. What marks it off, however, from their contention that schools reflect and contribute to the inequalities of an economic system, is its argument that, for the first time, a putative natural science of psychology was thrown into the fray to rescue a social system from its self-generated debilitating effects. Its lack of success in this task means that psychology is not a science and that the present woes experienced by Western industrial societies must be resolved by political and economic changes. Whether psychologists, as some sort of scientists, can play a part in these changes is a debatable question to which, having lived well off the old society now in decay, they have never addressed themselves.

BIBLIOGRAPHY

Abbott, J. H. In prison. *The New York Review of Books*, 1980, *27*(11), 34-37.

Abelson, W. D., Sigler, E. and DeBlasi, C. Effects of a four-year follow through program on economically disadvantaged children. *Journal of Educational Psychology*, 1974, *66*, 756-71.

Adams, I. Cameron, W., Hill, B., and Penz, P. *The real poverty report*. Edmonton: Hurtig, 1971.

Albee, G. W. The Protestant ethic, sex and psychotherapy. *American Psychologist*, 1977, *32*, 2, 150-61.

Alexander, M. Political repression in the U.S.A. *Canadian Dimension*, 1976, *11*(6), 16-22.

Amiel, B. The Ignorant Canadians Part 2. Solution: Educate only an elite. *Saturday Night*, 1976, *91*, 24-30.

Anderson, C. C. Clarifying what values? *Canadian Counsellor*, 1979, *14*(1), 36-40.

_____ . Some correlates of TV viewing. Unpublished paper, 1980.

_____ . The bogus science. *Canadian Journal of Education*, 1981, *6*(4), 8-22.

Andreski, S. *Prospect of a revolution in the U.S.A.* New York: Harper & Row, 1973.

Anglin, J. M., ed. *Beyond the Information given*. London: Allen and Unwin, 1974.

Arensberg, C. M. and A. Niehoff. *Introducing social change: A manual for Americans overseas*. Chicago: Aldine Publishing Company, 1964.

Armbruster, F. E. The more we spend, the less children learn. *The New York Times Magazine*, 1977 (August 28), 9-11, 53-54, 56, 60.

Armer, P. Attitudes towards intelligent machines. In E. A. Feigenbaum and J. Feldman, eds. *Computers and thought*. McGraw Hill, 1963.

Armor, D. J. The evidence on busing. *The Public Interest*, 1972, *28*, 90-128.

Aron, A. How social psychology can succeed: a response to Silverman. *Canadian Psychological Review*, 1979, *20*(1), 48-52.

Asbell, B. The outlawing of next year's cars. *The New York Times Magazine*, November 21, 1976, 9-11, 53-54, 56, 60.

Averch, H. J. et al. How effective is schooling? A critical synthesis and review of research findings. In D. M. Levine and M. J. Bane, eds. *The "inequality" controversy: schooling and distributive justice*. New York: Basic Books, 1975.

Bainton, R. H. Psychiatry and history: an examination of Erikson's *Young Man Luther*. *Religion in Life*, 1961, 450-78.

Bandura, A. Behaviour theory and the models of man. *American Psychologist*, 1974, 29(12), 859-69.

———— *Social learning theory*. Englewood Cliffs, New Jersey: Prentice-Hall, 1977.

————.The self system in reciprocal determinism. *American Psychologist*, 1978, 33(4), 344-58.

———— and R. H. Walters. *Social learning and personality development*. New York: Holt, Rinehart and Winston, 1963.

Baran, P. A. and P. M. Sweezy. *Monopoly capital*. New York: Monthly Review Press, 1966.

Barber, B. Resistance by scientists to scientific discovery. *Science*, 1961, 134, 569-602.

Bartlett, F. C. *Remembering*. Cambridge: Cambridge University Press, 1932.

Base, A., ed. *Marxian and post-Marxian political economy*. Harmondsworth: Penguin, 1975.

Becker, E. *The denial of death*. New York: Free Press, 1973.

Bell, D. *The end of ideology*. New York: Collier Books, 1962.

Belmont, L., Z. Stein and P. Zybert. Child spacing and birth order: effect on intellectual ability in two-child families. *Science*, 1978, 202, 995-96.

Berry, J. W. Social psychology: comparative, societal and universal. *Canadian Psychological Review*, 1978, 19(2), 93-104.

Bettelheim, B. *The informed heart: the human condition in modern society*. New York: Thames and Hudson, 1961.

Bevan, W. The sound of the wind that's blowing. *American Psychologist*, 1976, 31, 7, 481-91.

Birch, D., J. W. Atkinson, and K. Bongort. *Cognitive Views of human motivation*. New York: Academic Press, 1974.

Blackburn, R. and Cockburn, A., eds. *The incompatibles*. Hammondsworth: Penguin, 1967.

Blakemore, C. *Mechanics of the mind*. Cambridge, U.K.: Cambridge University Press, 1977.

Blaustein, A. I. Proposition 13 = Catch 22. *Harper's*, 1978, 257(1542), 18-22.

Block, J. H. Conceptions of sex-role: Some cross-cultural and longitudinal perspectives. *American Psychologist*, 1973, 28(6), 512-26.

————.Debatable conclusions about sex differences. *Contemporary Psychology*, 1976, 21(8), 517-20.

Bloom, B. S. *Alterable variables: The new direction in educational research*. Edinburgh: Scottish Council for Educational Research, 1979.

Boden, M. A. *Artificial intelligence and natural man*. Hassocks, Sussex: The Harvester Press, 1977.

————. *Piaget*. London: Fontana, 1979.

Boring, E. G. *A history of experimental psychology*. New York: Appleton-Century Crofts, 1929.

Bottomore, T. B. *Karl Marx: Early writings*. New York: McGraw-Hill, 1963.

Bowers, C. A. *The progressive educator and the depression: The radical years*. New York: Random House, 1969.

Bowles, S. and H. Gintis. *Schooling in capitalist America*. New York: Basic Books, 1976.

Brainerd, C. J. Cognitive development and concept learning: An interpretative review. *Psychological Bulletin*, 1977, 84(5), 919-39.

Braverman, H. *Labor and monopoly Capital*. New York: Monthly Review Press, 1974.

Broadbent, D. E. *Perception and communication*. London: Pergamon Press, 1958.

————. *Decision and stress*. London: Academic Press, 1971a.

_____. Relation between theory and application in psychology. In P. B. Warr et al. eds. *Psychology at work*. Harmondsworth, Middlesex: Penguin, 1971b.

_____. *In defence of empirical psychology*. London: Methuen, 1973.

Bronfenbrenner, U. *Two worlds of childhood: U.S. and U.S.S.R.* New York: Russell Sage Foundation, 1970.

Brown, G. and C. Desforges. Piagetian psychology and education: Time for revision. *British Journal of Educational Psychology*, 1977, *47*, 7-17.

Bruner, J. S. Personality dynamics and the process of perceiving. In R. R. Blake and G. V. Ramsey, eds. *Perception: An approach to personality*. New York: Ronald, 1951.

_____. *Toward a theory of instruction*. Cambridge, Massachusetts: Harvard University Press, 1966.

_____. Bad education. *Psychology Today*, 1970a, *4*(7), 51-54, 56-57, 70, 72, 74.

_____. Constructive cognitions. *Contemporary Pschology*, 1970b, *15*, 81-83.

_____. The process of education revisited. *Phi Deta Kappan*, 1971a, *53*, 18-21.

_____. *The relevance of education*. New York: Morton, 1971b.

_____. Poverty and childhood. *Oxford Review of Education*, 1973, *1*(1), 31-50.

_____. Psychology and the image of man. *Times Literary Supplement*, December 17, 1976, 1589-91.

_____, and R. R. Olver. Development of equivalence transformations in children. *Monographs of the Society for Research in Child Development*, 1963, *28*(2, Serial No. 112).

Brunswick, E. Scope and aspects of the behavior problem. In H. E. Gruber, K. R. Hammond and R. Jessor, eds. *Contemporary approaches to cognition*. Cambridge, Mass.: Harvard University Press, 1957.

Bryan, J. H. Children's cooperation and helping behaviors. In E. M. Hetherington, ed. *Review of Child Development Research*, vol. 5. Chicago: University of Chicago Press, 1975.

Buss, A. R. *A dialectical psychology*. New York: Irvington, 1979.

Campbell, D. T. On the conflicts between biological and social evolution and between psychology and moral tradition. *American Psychologist*, 1975, *30*, 12, 1103-26.

Carey, J. Life and death in liberal England. *The Sunday Times*, February 10, 1980, 42.

Carroll, J. B. How shall we study individual differences in cognitive abilities? Methodological and theological perspectives. *Intelligence*, 1978, *2*, 87-115.

Cartwright, D. Determinants of scientific process: The case of research on the risky shift. *American Psychologist*, 1973, *28*(3), 221-31.

Carver, S. A. Interests and alliances, *Harper's*, 1980, *261*(1562), 18-22.

Cattell, J. M. Mental tests and measurements. *Mind*, 1890, *15*, 373-80.

Cattell, R. B. Multivariate behavioral research and the integrative challenge. *Multivariate Behavior Research*, 1966, *1*, 4-23.

Caudill, H. M. American serfdom: The backward coal industry. *Atlantic Monthly*, 1978, *241*(6), 35-41.

Caute, D. *The great fear*. New York: Simon and Schuster, 1978.

Chess, S. Genesis of behavior disorders. In J. G. Howells, ed. *Modern perspectives in international child psychiatry*. New York: Bruner/Mazel, 1972.

Chomsky, N. Three models for the description of language. *IRE Transactions on Information Theory*, 1956, *IT-2*(3), 113-24.

_____. The case against B. F. Skinner. *The New York Review of Books*, 1971 *17*(11), 18-24.

Church, J. Psychology and the social order. *Annals of the New York Academy of Science*, 1976, *270*, 141-51.

Cicirelli, V. G., J. W. C. Evans, and J. S. Schiller. The impact of Head Start: A reply to the report analysis. *Harvard Educational Review*, 1970, *40*, 105-29.

Cirino, R. *Don't blame the people*. Los Angeles: Diversity Press, 1971.

Clarke, A. M. and A. D Clarke. *Early experience: Myth and evidence*. London: Open Books, 1976.

Cohen, D. K. and Garet, M. S. Reforming educational policy with applied social research. *Harvard Educational Review*, 1975, *45*, 1, 16-43.

Cole, M. *The story of Fabian socialism*. New York: Wiley, 1964.

Coles, R. Stricken Boston. *The New York Review of Books*, 1975, *22*(13), 39-42.

Coleman, J. S. Coleman on "The Coleman Report." *The Public Interest*, 1972, *28*, 127-28.

_____. The conception of equality of educational opportunity. In D. M. Levine and M. J. Bane, eds. *The "inequality" controversy: Schooling and distributive justice*. New York: Basic Books, 1975.

Collier, P. and D. Horowitz. *The Rockefellers: An American dynasty*. New York: New American Library, 1976.

Collins, R. *The credential society*. New York: Academic Press, 1979.

Constantineau, G. The myth of TV violence. *In Search*, 1978, *5*, 4, 2-9.

Cooke, H. and S. Stingle. Cooperative behavior in children. *Psychological Bulletin*, 1974, *84*, 913-17.

Craik, K. J. W. *The nature of explanation*. Cambridge: Cambridge University Press, 1943.

Crawford, C. George Washington, Abraham Lincoln and Arthur Jensen: Are they compatible? *American Psychologist*, 1979, *34*(8), 664-72.

Crews, F. American prophet. *The New York Review of Books*, 1975, *22*(16), 9-15.

Cronbach, L. J. Beyond the two disciplines of scientific psychology. *American Psychologist*, 1975, *30*(1), 116-27.

_____ and P. E. Meehl. Construct validity in psychological tests. *Psychological Bulletin*, 1955, *52*(4), 281-302.

Cummins, J. and Das, J. P. Cognitive processing and reading difficulties: A framework for research. *The Alberta Journal of Educational Research*, 1977, *23*, 4, 245-56.

Darlington, R. B. et al. Preschool programs and later school competence of children from low income families. *Science*, 1980, *208*, 202-204.

Das, J. P., Kirby, J. and Jarman, R. I. Simultaneous and successive syntheses: An alternative model for cognitive abilities. *Psychological Bulletin*, 1975, *82*, 87-103.

DeCharms, R. and Muir, M. Motivation: Social approaches. *Annual Review of Psychology*, 1978, *29*, 91-113.

Dennett, D. C. *Brainstorms: Philosophical essays on mind and psychology*. Montgomery, Vermont: Bradford Books, 1978.

Desforges, C. and D. Brown. The educational utility of Piaget: A reply to Shaver. *British Journal of Educational Psychology*, 1979, *49*, 277-81.

Detterman, D. K. Detterman's laws of individual differences research. In R. Sternberg and D. J. Detterman, eds. *Human intelligence: Perspectives on its theory and research*. New Jersey: Ablex, 1979.

Dreikers, R. *The challenge of child training*. New York: Hawthorn, 1972.

Drummond, H. You're okay, they're not. *Mother Jones Reprints*, 1978.

_____. Power. Madness and poverty. *Mother Jones*, 1980, *5*, 20-39.

Dunlap, J. W. Psychologists and the cold war. *American Psychologist*, 1955, *10*, 107-109.

Ebel, R. L. Some limitations of basic research in education. *Phi Delta Kappan*, 1967, *49*, 81-84.

Educational Testing Service. *Test scores and family income*. Princeton, New Jersey: Educational Testing Service, 1980.

Ehrenfeld, D. *The arrogance of humanism*. New York: Oxford University Press, 1978.

Ehrlich, P. *The population bomb*. New York: Ballentine, 1968.

Elkind, D. Wilhelm Reich—The psycho-analyst as revolutionary. *The New York Times Magazine*, 1971, (April 18), 25-27, 56-57, 62-65, 72-73.

Ellul, J. *Propaganda: The formation of men's attitudes*. New York: Vintage Books, 1973.

Elms, A. C. The crisis of confidence in social psychology. *American Psychologist*, 1975, *30*(10), 967-76.

English, D. The politics of porn. *Mother Jones*, 1980, *5*(1), 20-23, 43-44, 46-68.

Entwhistle, D. E. To dispel fantasies about fantasy based measures of achievement motivation. *Psychological Bulletin*, 1972, *77*(6), 377-91.

Erikson, E. H. *Identity and the life cycle*. New York: International Universities Press, 1959.

_____. *Childhood and society*. New York: Norton, 1963.

_____. *Ghandi's truth*. New York: Norton, 1969.

_____. *In search of common ground: Conversations with Erik H. Erikson and Huey Newton*. New York: Norton, 1973.

_____. *Dimensions of a new identity*. New York: Norton, 1974.

Estes, W. K. Learning theory and intelligence. *American Psychologist*, 1974, *29*(10), 740-49.

_____. Is human memory obsolete? *American Scientist*, 1980, *68*(1), 62-69.

Etzioni, A. Do as I say, not as I do. *The New York Times Magazine*. September 26, 1976, 44-46.

Eurich, A. C. and G. Kraetsch. A 50-year comparison of University of Minnesota freshmen's reading performance. *Journal of Educational Psychology*, 1982, *74*(5), 660-65.

Evans, C. *The mighty micro*. London: Gollanz, 1979.

Ewen, S. *Captains of consciousness*. New York: McGraw-Hill, 1976.

Eysenck, H. J. The influence of schools. *Books and Bookmen*, 1979, *24*(12), 48-49.

_____. Behaviorism. *Books and Bookmen*, 1979a, *25*(2), 40-41.

Fallows, J. The tests and the "brightest": How fair are the college boards? *The Atlantic*, 1980, *245*(2), 37-48.

Feifer, G. Russian disorders. *Harper's*. 1981, *262*, 41-55.

Ferrante, A. The expendable Canadians. *McLean's*, 1977 (November), 74-76.

Ferster, C. B., and B. F. Skinner. *Schedules of reinforcement*. New York: Appleton-Century-Crofts, 1957.

Feyerabend, P. *Against method: Outline of an anarchistic theory of knowledge*. London: New Left Books, 1975.

Firkowska, A., et al. Cognitive development and social policy. *Science*, 1978, *200*, 1357-62.

Frady, M. Black power now. *The New York Review of Books*, 1980, *27*(9), 15-19.

Friedenberg, E. *The disposal of liberty and other industrial wastes*. New York: Anchor, 1976.

Frijda, N. Simulation of human long term memory. *Psychological Bulletin*, 1972, *77*(1), 1-31.

Froome, S. *Why Tommy isn't learning*. London: Tom Stacey Books, 1970.

Gagne, R. M. Military training and principles of learning. *American Psychologist*, 1962a, *17*, 83-91.

_____. *The conditions of learning*. New York: Holt, Rinehart and Winston, 1962b.

Galbraith, J. K. *The affluent society*. New York: Houghton Mifflin, 1958.

_____. *The new industrial state*. Boston: Houghton Mifflin, 1967.

_____. *Economics, peace and laughter*. New York: Signet Books, 1972.

_____. *Economics and the public purpose*. New York: Signet Books, 1975.

————. *Annals of an abiding liberal*. Boston: Houghton Mifflin, 1979.

————. *Two pleas at Berkeley. The New York Review of Books*, 1980, 27(12), 25-26.

Galton, F. *Inquiries into human faculty and its development*. London: Dent, 1883.

Galvin, R. M. Psychology: There are other therapists at work. *The New York Times*, August 15, 1977, E7.

Geng, V. Requiem for the women's movement. *Harper's*, 1976, 253(1518), 45-56.

George, S. *How the other half dies*. Harmondsworth, Middlesex: Penguin, 1976.

Gergen, K. J. Social psychology as history. *Journal of Personality and Social Psychology*, 1973, 28(2), 309-20.

Gibson, J. J. *The senses considered as perceptual systems*. Boston: Houghton Mifflin, 1966.

Gibson, E. J., and H. Levin. *The psychology of reading*. Cambridge, Massachusetts: MIT Press, 1975.

Gilmor, T. M. Locus of control as a mediator of adaptive behavior in children and adolescents. *Canadian Psychological Review*, 1978, 19(1), 1-26.

Giorgi, A. *Psychology as a human science*. New York: Harper & Row, 1970.

Glaser, R. Components of a psychology of instruction: Towards a science of design. *Review of Educational Research*, 1976, 46(1), 1-24.

————. Instructional psychology: Past, present, future. *American Psychologist*, 1982, 37(3), 292-305.

Golinkoff, R. A developing theory: Jean Piaget's ideas, 1965-1980. *Contemporary Psychology*, 1982, 27(2), 102-104.

Gonick, C. Socialism and the economics of growthmanship. In La Pierre, et al., eds. *Essays on the Left*. Toronto: McClelland and Stewart, 1979.

Goodenough, F. L. *Mental testing*. London: Staples Press, 1950.

Goodman, W. *The committee*. Baltimore, Maryland: Penguin Books, 1969.

Gorz, A. *Strategy for labor*. Boston: Beacon Press, 1968.

Gould, S. J. Jensen's last stand. *The New York Review of Books*, 1980, 28(7), 38-44.

Gourlay, N. Heredity vs. environment: The effects of genetic variation with age. *British Journal of Educational Psychology*. 1978, 48, 1-21.

Gray, J. H. *Pavlov*. London: Fontana/Collins, 1979.

Greenfield, P. M. On culture and conservation. In Bruner, J. S., ed. *Studies in cognitive growth*. New York: Wiley, 1966.

Gregory, R. The brain: An engineering problem. *Discovery*, 1962, 22(1), 22-25.

Grinder, R. E. What 200 years tells us about professional priorities in educational psychology. *Educational Psychologist*. 1978, 12, 284-89.

Gross, M. L. *The psychological society*. New York: Random House, 1978.

Gruber, H. E., K. R. Hammond, and R. Jessor, eds. *Contemporary approaches to cognition*. Cambridge: Harvard University Press, 1957.

Gulliksen, H. Looking back and ahead in psychometrics. *American Psychologist*, 1974, 29, 4, 223-32.

Gurin, P., G. Gurin, R. C. Lao, and M. Beattie. Internal-external control in the dynamics of Negro youth. *Journal of Social Issues*, 1969, 25, 29-53.

Gutmann, D. Erik Erikson's America. *Commentary*, 1974, 58, 60-64.

Hacker, A. *The end of the American era*. New York: Athaneum Press, 1971.

Halsey, A. M., A. F. Heath, and J. M. Ridge. *Origins and destinations: Family, class and education in modern Britain*. London: Oxford University Press, 1978.

Hapgood, D. *The screwing of the average man*. New York: Doubleday, 1974.

Harper, L. V. The young as a source of stimuli controlling caretaker behavior. *Developmental Psychology*, 1971, 7, 71-78.

Harre, R. Blueprint for a new science. In N. Armistead, ed. *Reconstructing social psychology*. Harmondsworth, Middlesex: Penguin, 1974.

_____ and P. F. Secord. *The explanation of social behavior*. Oxford: Blackwell, 1972.

Hartshorne, H. and May, M. *Studies in the nature of character*. New York: Macmillan, 1928-1930.

Hazlitt, V. Children's thinking. *British Journal of Psychology*, 1930, *20*, 354-61.

Hearnshaw, L. S. *Cyril Burt, psychologist*. London: Hodder and Stoughton, 1979.

Hebb, D. O. What psychology is about. *American Psychologist*, 1974, *29*(2), 71-79.

Heilbroner, R. *The future as history*. New York: Harper & Row, 1960.

Heron, C. Punching the clock. *Canadian Dimension*, 1979, *14*(3), 26-29.

Herrnstein, R. J. The evolution of behaviorism. *American Psychologist*, 1977a, *32*(8), 593-603.

_____. Doing what comes naturally: A reply to Professor Skinner. *American Psychologist*, 1977b, *32*(12), 1013-16.

Hetherington, E. M. and Parke, R. D., eds. *Contemporary readings in child psychology*. New York: McGraw-Hill, 1977.

Hilton, J. and J. Shirley. The interrogators. *Sunday Times*, August 10, 1980, 13.

Hitchcock, J. Comes the cultural revolution. *The New York Times Magazine*, 1979 (July 27), 4-5, 40, 52.

Hobsbawm, E. J. *The age of capital*. London: Weidenfeld and Nicolson, 1975.

Hodgson, G. Do schools make a difference? In D. M. Levine and M. J. Bane, eds. *The "inequality" controversy: schooling and distributive justice*. New York: Basic Books, 1975.

_____. *America in our time*. New York: Doubleday, 1976.

_____. *All things to all men: The false promise of the modern American presidency*. New York: Viking Press, 1980.

Hoffmann, S. The crisis in the West. *The New York Review of Books*, 1980, *27*(12), 41-48.

Hofstadter, R., ed. *The progressive movement*. Englewood Cliffs: Prentice-Hall, 1963.

_____. *Anti-intellectualism in American life*. New York: Vintage Books, 1966.

_____. Reflections on violence in the United States. In R. Hofstadter and M. Wallace, eds. *American violence: A documentary history*. New York: Vintage Books, 1971.

Hogan, R. *Personality theory: The personalogical tradition*. Englewood Cliffs: Prentice-Hall, 1976.

Hoggart, R and Golden, A. E. *Rumours of war*. Toronto: New Press, 1971.

Hollingshead, A. B. and Redlich, F. C. *Social class and mental illness: A commodity study*. New York: Wiley, 1958.

Horowitz, D. *Student*. New York: Ballantine Books, 1962.

Horowitz, G. Conservatism, liberalism and socialism in Canada: An interpretation. *The Canadian Journal of Economics and Political Science*, 1966, *32*(2), 143-71.

Hottinger, A. The rich Arab states in trouble. *The New York Review of Books*, 1980, *27*(4), 23-24.

Hull, C. L. The conflicting psychologies of learning: A way out. *Psychological Review*, 1934, *43*, 491-515.

_____. *Principles of behavior*. Englewood Cliffs, New Jersey: Prentice-Hall, 1943.

Hunt, J. M. *Intelligence and experience*. New York: The Ronald Press, 1961.

Hurvitz, N. Psychotherapy as a means of social control. *Journal of Consulting and Clinical Psychology*, 1973, *40*, 232-39.

Hutt, C. *Males and females*. Harmondsworth, Middlesex: Penguin, 1972.

Hyman, I. A. Psychology, education, and schooling: Social policy implications in the lives of children and youth. *American Psychologist*, 1974, *34*(10), 1024-29.

Ingleby, D. The job psychologists do. In N. Armistead, ed. *Reconstructing social psychology*. Harmondsworth, Middlesex: Penguin, 1974.

Isaacs, S. *The children we teach*. London: The University of London Press, 1970.

Jackson, G. B. Towards expediting the resolution of debates in the social sciences. *Educational Psychologist*, 1978, *12*, 324-31.

Jacoby, R. *Social amnesia*. Boston: Beacon Press, 1975.

James, M. and Jongeward, D. *Born to win*. Reading, Mass.: Addison-Wesley, 1976.

Janzen, H. L. and D. Beeken. An analysis of the applicability of the locus of control construct. *The Alberta Journal of Educational Research*, 1973, *19*, 295-302.

Jarman, R. F. and J. P. Das. Simultaneous and successive synthesis and intelligence. *Intelligence*, 1977, *1* 194-227.

Jay, M. *The dialectical imagination*. London: Heinneman, 1973.

Jencks, C. A reappraisal of the most controversial educational document of our time. *The New York Times Magazine*, August 10, 1969, 13-14, 34, 36-38.

_____ *et al. Inequality*. New York: Basic Books, 1972.

Jenkins, P. Mrs. Thatcher survives her first winter intact. *The Guardian*, 1980, *122*(16), 4.

Jensen, A. R. How much can we boost IQ and scholastic achievement? *Harvard Educational Review*, 1969, *39*, 1-123.

_____ *. Genetics and education*. London: Methuen, 1972.

Joncich, G. *The sane positivist: A biography of Edward L. Thorndike*. Middletown, Connecticut: Wesleyan University Press, 1968.

Jones, L. V. Achievement test scores in mathematics and science. *Science*, 1981, *213* (July 24), 412-16.

Kaiser, R. G. *Russia: The power and the people*. New York: Pocket Books, 1976.

Kamin, L. J. Jensen's last stand. *Psychology Today*, 1980, *13*(9), 117-18, 120.

Kanfer, F. H. Personal control, social control and altruism: Can society survive the age of individualism? *American Psychologist*, 1979, *34*(3), 231-39.

Kaplan, M. *Essential works of Pavlov*. New York: Bantam Books, 1966.

Karabel, J. The reasons why. *The New York Review of Books*, 1979, *26*, 1, 22-27.

Karier, C. J. Liberalism and the quest for orderly change. In R. Dale et al. *Schooling and Capitalism*. London: Routledge and Kegan Paul, 1976a, 90-97.

_____ *. Testing for order and control in the corporate liberal state. In R. Dale, et al., *Schooling and Capitalism*. London: Routledge and Kegan Paul, 1976b, 128-41.

Kerr, D. Hollywood massage parlour. *Canadian Dimension*, 1977, *12*, 4, 52-53.

Kline, M. *Why Johnny can't add*. New York: Vintage, 1974.

Koch, S. Psychology as a science. In S. C. Brown, ed. *Philosophy as psychology*. London: Macmillan, 1974.

_____ *. Psychology and the future. *American Psychologist*, 1978, *33*, 637-39.

Koestler, A. *The ghost in the machine*. London: Hutchinson, 1967.

Kohlberg, L. The development of children's orientation towards a moral order: Sequence in the development of moral thought. *Vita Humana*, 1963, *6*, 11-33.

_____ *. A cognitive-developmental analysis of children's sex-role concepts and attitudes. In E. E. Maccoby, ed. *Development of sex differences*. Stanford, California: Stanford University Press, 1966.

_____ *. Moral education in the schools; A developmental view. In R. E. Muus, ed. *Adolescent behavior and society: A book of readings*. New York: Random House, 1971a.

_____ *. Stages of moral education. In C. M. Beck, B. S. Crittenden, and E. V. Sullivan, eds. *Moral education: Interdisciplinary approaches*. Toronto: University of Toronto Press, 1971b.

_____ and C. Gilligan. The adolescent as a philosopher: The discovery of self in a post conventional world. In J. R. Kagan and R. Coles, eds. *Twelve to sixteen: Early adolescence*. New York: Norton, 1972.

Krasner, L. The future and the past in the behaviorism-humanism dialogue. American Psychologist, 1978, *33*(9), 799-804.

Kuhn, T. S. *The structure of scientific revolutions*. Chicago: University of Chicago Press, 1962.

Kurtines, W. and E. B. Grief. The development of moral thought: Review and evaluation of Kohlberg. *Psychological Bulletin*, 1974, *81*(8), 453-70.

Ladd, G. T. President's address. *Psychological Review*, 1894, *1*(1), 1-22.

Lane, R. E. *Political ideology*. Glencoe, Illinois: Free Press, 1967.

Lasch, C. Inequality and education. In D. M. Levine and M. J. Bane, eds. *The inequality controversy*. New York: Basic Books, 1975.

_____ . *The culture of narcissism*. New York: Warner/Norton, 1979.

Lashley, K. S. and Ball, J. Spinal conduction and kinaesthetic sensitivity in maze habit. *Journal of Comparative Psychology*, 1929, *9*, 71-106.

Laswell, H. D. The triple-appeal principle: A contribution of psychoanalysis to political and social science. *American Journal of Sociology*, 1932, *37*(4), 523-38.

Lawson, R. A. *The future of independent liberalism 1930-1941*. New York: G. P. Putnam's, 1971.

Laxer, J. and R. Laxer. *The liberal idea of Canada*. Toronto: Lorimer, 1977.

_____ and A. Martin. *The big tough expensive job*. Don Mills, Ontario: Press Porcepic, 1976.

Layzer, D. Science or superstition? (A physical scientist looks at the IQ controversy). *Cognition*, 1972, *1* 265-95.

Lazarus, A. A. Has behavior therapy outlived its usefulness? *American Psychologist*, 1977, *32*(7), 550-54.

Lefcourt, H. M. The function of the illusions of control and freedom. *American Psychologist*, 1973, *28*(5), 417-25.

Lesgold, A. M., et al. *Cognitive psychology and instruction*. New York: Plenum Press, 1978.

Levine, M. Scientific method and the adversary model. *American Psychologist*, 1974, *20*(4), 661-67.

Levitt, K. Towards decolonisation: Canada and Quebec. *The Canadian Forum*, 1972, *51*(3), 2-11.

Lewis, A. *Portrait of a decade*. New York: Bantam Books, 1965.

Lewis, P. *The fifties*. London: Heinemann, 1978.

Leys, S. *Chinese shadows*. Harmondsworth, Middlesex: Penguin, 1978.

Linstone, H. A. On discounting the future. *Technological Forecasting and Social Change*, 1973, *4*, 335-38.

Loye, D. Towards a more knowledge future. *APA Monitor*, 1977, *8*(1), 4-5.

Lundberg, F. *The rich and the super-rich*. New York: Bantam, 1969.

Luria, A. R. *The working brain*. London: Penguin, 1973.

Lynn, R. Comprehensives and equality: The quest for the unattainable. In C. B. Cox and A. E. Dyson, eds. *Black Paper Two*. London: The Critical Quarterly Press, 1970.

Maccoby, E. E. and C. N. Jacklin. *The psychology of sex differences*. Stanford, California: Stanford University Press, 1974.

MacIntyre, A. The irrelevance of the Church of England. *The Listener*, 1958, *59*, 1055-56, 1058-59.

Mackenzie, B. D. *Behaviourism and the limits of scientific method*. London: Routledge and Kegan Paul, 1977.

Macpherson, C. B. *The real world of democracy*. Toronto: C.B.C. Publications, 1965.

_____ . *The political theory of possessive individualism*. London: Oxford University Press, 1962.

MacRae, D. G. *Weber*. London: Woburn Press, 1974.

Maeroff, G. I. The unfavored gifted few. *The New York Times Book Review*, August 21, 1977, 30-32, 72-76.

Magdoff, H. *The age of imperialism*. New York: Monthly Review Press, 1969.

Maguire, T. O. and Haig, B. Problems of control in nonexperimental and educational research. *Alberta Journal of Education Research*, 1976, *22*(4), 289-96.

Mahoney, M. Reflections on the cognitive-learning trend in psychotherapy. *American Psychologist*, 1977, *32*, 1, 5-13.

Marceau, J. Education and social mobility in France. In F. Parkin, ed. *The social analysis of class structure*. London: Tavistock Press, 1974.

Marcia, J. E. Development and validation of ego-identity status. *Journal of Personality and Social Psychology*, 1966, *3*(5), 551-58.

Marcus, S. *Engels, Manchester and the working class*. London: Weidenfeld and Nicolson, 1974.

Marcuse, H. *An essay on liberation*. Boston: Beacon Press, 1969.

Martin, B. Parent-child relations. In F. D. Horowitz, ed. *Review of child development research*. Chicago: University of Chicago Press, 1975.

McClelland, D. C. *The achieving society*. New York: Van Nostrand, 1961.

———. *Power: The inner experience*. New York: Irvington, 1975.

———, et al. *The achievement motive*. New York: Appleton-Century-Crofts, 1953.

McCormack, T. The Protestant ethic and the spirit of socialism. *British Journal of Sociology*, 1969, *20*(3), 266-76.

McGuire, W. J. The yin and yang of process in social psychology: Seven koan. *The Journal of Personality and Social Psychology*, 1973, *26*(3), 446-56.

McKeachie, W. J. Instructional psychology. *Annual Review of Psychology*, 1974, *25*, 161-93.

McKinney, F. Fifty years of psychology. *American Psychologist*, 1976, *31*(12), 834-42.

McLauchlan, D. Modifying the task strategies of impulsive children. (Unpublished doctoral dissertation.) Edmonton: University of Alberta, 1977.

McLeish, J. *The science of behaviour*. London: Barrie and Rockliff, 1963.

———. *Soviet psychology*. London: Methuen, 1975.

———. Behaviourism is also a humanism. *Canadian Journal of Education*, 1976, *1*(4), 69-81.

Medawar, P. B. Is the scientific paper a fraud? In D. Edge, eds. *Experiment*. London: British Broadcasting Corporation, 1964.

———. Science and literature. *Encounter*, 1969, *32*(11), 15-23.

———. Unnatural science. *The New York Review of Books*, February 3, 1977, 13-18.

Meyer, P. Entangled freedoms. *Harper's*, 1980, *260*(1561), 37-56.

Michels, R. *Political parties*. London: Eden and Cedar Paul, 1915.

Miles, M. W. *The radical probe: The logic of the student rebellion*. New York: Athaneum, 1971.

Milgram, S. *Obedience to authority: An experimental view*. New York: Harper & Row, 1974.

Miller, G. Human memory and the storage of information. *IRE Transactions on Information Theory*, 1956, *II-2*(3), 129-38.

———. Psychology as a means of promoting human welfare. *American Psychologist*, 1969, *24*(12), 1063-75.

Miller, G. A. The magical number seven, plus or minus two. *Psychological Review*, 1956, *63*, 81-97.

———, E. Galanter, and K. H. Pribram. *Plans and the structure of behavior*. New York: Holt, 1960.

Mills, C. W. *Sociology and pragmatism*. New York: Oxford University Press, 1966.

Mills, J. A. A summary of criticism of Skinner's early theory of learning. *Canadian Psychological Review*, 1978, *19*, 215-23.

Milowe, F. D. and R. S. Lowire. The child's role in the battered child syndrome. *Journal of Pediatrics*, 1964, *65*, 1079-81.

Mintz, M. and Cohen, J. S. *American Inc.* New York: Dell, 1971.

Mischel, M. A. A social-learning view of sex differences in behavior. In E. E. Maccoby, ed. *The development of sex differences in behavior*. Stanford, California: Stanford University Press, 1966.

Mitchell, J. *Woman's estate*. Harmondsworth, Middlesex: Penguin, 1971.

Mixon, D. If you won't deceive, what can you do? In N. Armistead, ed. *Reconstructing social psychology*. Harmondsworth, Middlesex: Penguin, 1974.

Moynihan, D. P. Equalising education: In whose benefit? In D. M. Levine and M. J. Bane, eds. *The "inequality" controversy: Schooling and distributive justice*. New York: Basic Books, 1975.

Neisser, U. *Cognitive psychology*. New York: Appleton-Century-Crofts, 1967.

_____ . Self-knowledge and psychological knowledge: Teaching psychology from a cognitive point of view. *Educational Psychologist*, 1975, *11*(3), 158-70.

_____ . *Cognition and reality*. San Francisco: Freedman, 1976.

Newell, A. You can't play twenty questions with nature and win. In W. G. Chase, ed. *Visual Information Processing*. New York: Academic Press, 1973.

Newfield, J. and Greenfield, J. *A populist manifesto*. New York: Praeger, 1972.

Nyquist, E. B. and G. R. Hawes. *Open education: A source book for parents and teachers.* New York: Bantam Books, 1972.

Odom, R. D. A perceptual account of decalage relations. In L. S. Siegel and C. J. Brainerd, eds. *Alternatives to Piaget*. New York: Academic Press, 1978.

Okin, S. *Women in western political thought*. Princeton: Princeton University Press, 1979.

Opton E. A psychologist takes a closer look at the recent landmark Larry P. opinion. *A.P.A. Monitor*, 1979, *10*(12),1, 4.

Osgoode, C. *Method and theory in experimental psychology*. New York: Oxford University Press, 1953.

Paivio, A. Concerning dual coding and simultaneous-successive processing. *Canadian Psychological Review*, 1976, *17*, 1, 69-72.

Park, C. An investigation of an aspect of reasoning. (Unpublished doctoral dissertation.) Edmonton: University of Alberta, 1976.

Pearson, K. *The grammar of science*. London: Adam and Charles Black, 1892.

Peter, K. A. Childhood and adolescent socialization among Hutterites. In K. Ishwaran, ed. *Childhood and adolescence in Canada*. New York: McGraw-Hill Ryerson, 1979.

Petronovich, L. Probabilistic functionalism: A conception of research method. *American Psychologist*, 1979. *34*(5), 373-90.

Pettigrew, B. K., et al. *Busing: A review of "the evidence." The Public Interest*, 1973, *30*, 80-118.

Phares, E. J. and Lamiell, J. T. Personality. *Annual Review of Psychology*, 1977, *28*, 113-40.

Phillips, D. C. and M. Kelly. Hierarchical theories of development in education and psychology. *Harvard Educational Review*, 1975, *45*(3), 351-75.

Piaget, J. Intellectual evolution from adolescence to adulthood. *Human Development*, 1972, *15*, 1-12.

Pines, M. *Revolution in learning*. New York: Harper & Row, 1967.

_____ . A head start in the nursery. *Psychology Today*, 1979, *13*(4), 56-57, 59-60, 63-64, 67-68.

Platt, J. R. Strong inference. *Science*, 1964, *146*, 347-53.

_____ . Man and indeterminacies. *Perspectives in Biology and Medicine*, 1966, *10*(1), 67-80.

_____ . Social traps. *American Psychologist*, 1973, *28*(8), 641-51.

Porter, J. *The measure of Canadian society: Education, equality, and opportunity.* Toronto: Gage, 1979.

Posner, M. I. and McLean, J. P. Review of Neisser's Cognition and Reality. *Contemporary Psychology*, 1977, *22*, 7, 481-82.

Postman, N. Order in the classroom. *The Atlantic*, 1979, *244*, 3, 35-38.

Pratt, L. The politics of Syncrude: Selling out. *The Canadian Forum*, 1976, *55*, 3-10, 13-17.

Preston, R. J. The development of self-control in the Eastern Cree life cycle. In K. Ishwaran, ed. *Childhood and adolescence in Canada.* New York: McGraw-Hill Ryerson, 1979.

Pyke, E. R. *Human documents of the age of the Forsythes.* London: Allen & Unwin, 1969.

Rapaport, A. Why behaviourism failed. *Queen's Quarterly*, 1978/79, *85*, 659-63.

Rapaport, R. The dark side of diesel chic. *Mother Jones*, 1980, *5*(2), 62-65.

Reitman, W. R. *Cognition and thought.* New York: Wiley, 1965.

Robertson, H. *Grass roots.* Toronto: Lorimer, 1973.

Robertson, J. Impressions and comments. *Scottish education looks ahead.* Edinburgh: W. & R. Chambers, 1969.

Rosenhan, D. L. On being sane in insane places. *Science*, 1973, *179*, 250-58.

Rotter, J. B. Generalized expectances for internal versus external control of reinforcement. *Psychological Monographs*, 1966, *80* (Whole No. 609).

_____ . A new scale for the measurement of interpersonal trust. *Journal of Personality*, 1967, *35*, 516-65.

_____ . External control and internal control. *Psychology Today*, 1971, *5*(1), 37-42, 58-59.

_____ . Interpersonal trust, trustworthiness and gullibility. *American Psychologist*, 1980, *35*(1), 1-7.

Rubinstein, E. Paradoxes of student protests. *American Psychologist*, 1969, *24*, 1, 133-41.

Sampson, A. *The seven sisters.* New York: Bantam, 1976.

Sanford, T. Picking the president: Time to change the rules: A plea for conventions that really work. *The Atlantic* 1980, *246*(2), 29-33.

Sarbin, T. R. On the futility of the proposition that some people may be labelled "mentally ill." *Journal of Consulting Psychology*, 1967, *31*(5), 447-53.

Schiller, H. I. *Mass communications and American empire.* New York: A.M. Kelly, 1970.

Schrag, P. Education's romantic critics. *Saturday Review*, 1967 (February 18).

Schultz, D. P. The human subject in psychological research. *Psychological Bulletin*, 1969, *72*, 214-28.

Schur, E. *The awareness trap: Self-absorption instead of social change.* New York: Quadrangle/The New York Times Book Company, 1976.

Scribner, S. and M. Cole. Cognitive consequences of formal and informal education. *Science*, 1973, 182, 553-59.

Sears, R. Your ancients revisited: A history of child development. In E. M. Hetherington, ed. *Review of Child Development Research*, vol. 5. Chicago: University of Chicago Press, 1975.

Shayer, M. Has Piaget's construct of formal operational thinking any utility? *British Journal of Educational Psychology*, 1979, *49*, 265-75.

Siegel, L. S. and Brainerd, C., eds. *Alternatives to Piaget.* New York: Academic Press, 1978.

Silverman, I. Why social psychology fails. *Canadian Psychological Review*, 1977, *18*, 353-58.

Simon, H. A. Motivational and emotional controls of cognition. *Psychological Review*, 1967, *74*(1), 29-39.

————.*The sciences of the artificial*. Cambridge, Massachusetts: The M.I.T. Press, 1969.

————, and A. Newell. Information processing in computer and man. *American Scientist*, 1964, *52*, 281-300.

Skinner, B. F. *Science and human behavior*. New York: Macmillan, 1953.

————. *Beyond freedom and dignity*. New York: Bantam/Vintage, 1972.

————. *About behaviorism*. London: Cap, 1974.

————. The steep and thorny way to a science of behavior. *American Psychologist*, 1975, *35*, 42-49.

————. Herrenstein and the evolution of behaviorism. *American Psychologist*, 1977, *32*(12), 1013-16.

Skolnik, A. The myth of the vulnerable child. *Psychology Today*, 1978, *11*(9), 56-60, 65.

Smith, G. and T. James. The effects of preschool: Some American and British evidence. *Oxford Review of Education*, 1975, *1*(3), 223-40.

Smith, K. U. and M.F. Smith. *Cybernetic principles of learning and educational design*. New York: Holt, Rinehart, and Winston, 1966.

Smith, M. S. and J. S. Bissell. Report analysis: The impact of Head Start. *Harvard Educational Review*, 1970, *40*, 51-104.

Smith, R. I. *The psychopath in society*. New York: Academic Press, 1978.

Soames, M. *Clementine Churchill*. London: Cassell, 1979.

Spearman, C. *The nature of "intelligence" and the principles of cognition*. London: Macmillan, 1923.

Spence, K. W. The relation of learning theory to the technology of education. *Harvard Educational Review, 1959, 29*(2), 84-95.

Sperry, R. W. Hemispheric disconnection and unity in conscious awareness. *American Psychologist, 1968, 23*(10), 723-33.

————. Science and the problem of values. *Perspectives in Biology and Medicine*, 1972, *16*, 115-30.

————. Bridging science and values: A unifying view of mind and brain. *American Psychologist*, 1977, *32*(1), 237-45.

Staub, E. *The development of prosocial behavior in children*. New York: General Learning Press, 1975.

Sternberg, R. J. Component processes in analogical reasoning. *Psychological Review*, 1977, *84*, 353-78.

————. Componential investigations of human intelligence. In A. M. Lesgold, ed. *Cognitive psychology and instruction*. New York: Plenum Press, 1978.

————. Isolating the components of intelligence. *Intelligence*, 1978b, *2*(2), 117-28.

————. Stalking the I.Q. quark. *Psychology Today*, 1979a, *13*(4), 42, 45, 47, 49-50.

————. The nature of mental abilities. *American Psychologist*, 1979b, *34*(3), 214-30.

————. and B. Rifkin. The development of analogical reasoning processes. *Journal of Experimental Child Psychology*, 1979, *27*, 195-232.

Stevenson, M. The outline of history. *Harper's*, 1960, *260*, 1557, 85-86.

Sullivan, E. V. *Kohlberg's structionalism: A critical appraisal*. Toronto: The Ontario Institute for Studies in Education, Monograph Series 15, 1977.

Swift, J. and J. Kuyek. Does Bell hold all the chips? *The Last Post*, 1980, *7*(7), 37-41.

Szamuely, T. Comprehensive inequality. In C. B. Cox and A. E. Dyson, eds. *Black paper two*. London: The Critical Quarterly Society, 1969.

Szasz, T. S. *The myth of mental illness*. New York: Perennial Library, 1974.

Tate, E. D. Viewer's perceptions of selected television programs. In J. V. LaMarsh, ed. *Report of the Royal Commission on Violence in the Communications Industry*, vol. 6. Toronto: Queen's Printer for Ontario, 1977.

Tavris, C. The end of the I. Q. slump. *Psychology Today*, 1976, *9*(11), 69-75.
Thorndike, E. L. *An introduction to the theory of mental and social measurements*. New York: Science Press, 1904.
————. *Human learning*. New York: Century, 1931.
————. *Human nature and the social order*. Cambridge, Massachusetts: M.I.T. Press, 1949.
Thurow, L. Education and economic equality. In D. M. Levine and M. J. Bane, eds. *The inequality controversy: Schooling and distributive justice*. New York: Basic Books, 1975.
Toynbee, Philip. The language of inequality. In R. Blackburn and A. Cockburn, eds. *The incompatibles: Trade union military and the consensus*. London: Penguin, 1967.
Traub, R. Importance of problem heterogeneity to programmed instruction. *Journal of Educational Psychology*, 1966, *56*, 11, 54-60.
Travis, L. D. Political economy, social learning and activism: Toward a theory of educational turmoil. (Unpublished doctoral dissertation.) Edmonton: University of Alberta, 1975.
————. Hinterland schooling and branch-plant psychology: Educational psychology in Canada today. *Canadian Journal of Education*, 1979, *4*, 4, 24-42.
Trivers, R. L. The evolution of reciprocal altruism. *The Quarterly Review of Biology*, 1971, *46*(4), 35-57.
Tuveson, E. L. *Redeemer nation: The idea of America's milennial role*. Chicago: University of Chicago Press, 1968.
Unger, R. K. Towards a redefinition of sex and gender. *American Psychologist*, 1979, *34*(1), 1085-94.
Varenne, H. La vie en Appleton. *Psychology Today*, 1978, *11*, 9, 66-74.
Vernon, P. E., R. A. Ryba, and R. J. Lang. Simultaneous and successive processing: An attempt at replication. *Canadian Journal of Behavioural Science*, 1978, *10*(1), 1-15.
Wachtel, Paul L. Investigation and its discontents: Some constraints on progress in psychological research. *American Psychologist*, 1980, *35*(5), 399-408.
Wason, P. C. and P. W. Johnson-Laird. *The psychology of reasoning*. London: Batsford, 1972.
Watson, J. B. *Behaviorism*. Chicago: University of Chicago Press, 1924.
————. *Psychological care of infant and child*. New York: Norton, 1928.
Watson, J. D. *The double helix*. London: Weidenfeld and Nicolson, 1968.
Weimer, W. B. Review of Neisser's *Cognition and Reality*. *Contemporary Psychology*, 1977, *22*(7), 483-84.
Weiner, B. D., ed. *Achievement motivation: From mechanism to cognition*. Chicago: Markham, 1972.
Weinstein, J. *The decline of socialism in America*. New York: Vintage Books, 1967.
White, M. and J. Duker. Suggested standards for children's samples. *American Psychologist*, 1973, *28*, 700-703.
White, R. A. A limit to the application of learning hierarchices. *Australian Journal of Education*, 1973, *17*(2), 153-56.
White, R. T. and R. M. Gagne. Past and future research on learning hierarchies. *Educational Psychologist*, 1974, *11*(1), 19-28.
Whyte, W. H. *The organization man*. New York: Doubleday, 1957.
Williams, L. P. *Michael Faraday*. London: Chapman, 1965.
Williams, Raymond. *May day manifesto*. London: Penguin, 1968.
Wills, G. *Nixon Agonistes*. New York: Mentor Book, 1970.
Wilson, J. *Philosophy and educational research*. London: National Foundation for Educational Research in England and Wales, 1972.

Wispe, L. and J. N. Thompson. The war between the words: Biological versus social evolution and some related issues. *American Psychologist*, 1976, *31* (5), 341-47.

Yankelovich, D. Why Nixon won. *The New York Review of Books,* 1972, *19* (9), 7.

Yinger, J. et al. *Middle start.* New York: Cambridge University Press, 1974.

Zajonc, R. B. Family configuration and intelligence. *Science, 1976, 192,* 227-36.

————, and J. Bargh. Birth order, family size and decline of SAT scores. *American Psychologist*, 1980, *35* (7), 662-68.

Zener, K. The significance of behavior accompanying conditioned salivary secretion for theories of the conditioned reflex. *American Journal of Psychology*, 1937, *50*, 384-403.

Zigler, E. A developmental psychologist's view of operation babylift. *American Psychologist*, 1976, *31* (5), 329-40.

————. The effectiveness of Head Start: Another look. *Educational Psychologist*, 1978, *13*, 71-77.

Zimbardo, P. G. On the ethics of intervention in human psychological research: With special reference to the Stanford prison experiment. *Cognition*, 1973, *2*, 2, 243-56.

————.The age of indifference, *Psychology Today*, 1980, *14*, 3, 70-76.

INDEX

Subject Index

abilities: as "ghosts," 91; sex differences in, 114-15; processes and behaviour (links), 91
accommodation, 13, 37, 39
achievement, 3, 25, 64, 75; educational, 3, 25
acid rain, 23
activists, 9; as good for business, 114
adaptation, 13, 37
Adler, A., 118
admission of error: advantages of, 111
Afghanistan, 108
agencies of mass persuasion, 16; and cognition, 16
aggression, 97; and dental repairs, 97
Albee, G., 100; assessment of some of his views, 100-104
Allport, G., 55
altruism, 59, 60-62, 118; and trust, 61
American: character, 55; dream, 8, 52; economy, 57; Federation of Teachers, 9; industrial life, 100; past (erroneous notions about), 59-60; politics (and bossism, machines, etc.), 52-53; problems with class, 103; *Teacher* (periodical), 9
amplified powers, 25
analogical reasoning, 70
anarchistic approach to knowledge, 121
animals: cats, rats, pigeons, 8-9
anticipation: and avoidance of trouble, 88
anti-clerical materialism, 6
anti-communism: and liberal consensus, 10; in curricula, 10; research grants and, 10
anti-educational environment, 33

artificial intelligence, (AI), 18, 19, 21; and computers against dehumanization, 18; programs, 21
assimilation, 13, 37, 39;
attainment: conditions affecting, 40
authoritative voices, 86
authorities (superordinate), 100-101
authority, 18, 59, 100; helplessness and, 18; distrust of, 59
automation, 23-24, 35
autonomous man, 8

Bandura, A.: and aggression, 97; criticism of recent work, 88; infinite regression of causes, 97; reciprocal determinism, 89
Barnard, H., 2
battering (child): and caretakers, 114
behaviour: influence of context on, 21
behaviourism: and educators, 8; and J. B. Watson, 6, 7; and reform, 66; logical and empirical flaws of, 8; cognitivists and (differences), 81-82; displacement of, 8
behaviouristic psychologists, 6
behaviourist-materialist principles, 89
behaviourists, 65
behaviour modification, 84, 98, 123-24
Binet, A., 98
biochemical influences on behaviour: denial of, 114; C. Hutt and, 117
birth order effect, 69; Zajonc and Bargh and, 69; and SAT scores, 69
birth rate, 120
blacks: American, 9, 27, 64, 65, 66; and whites (differences), 66

tional science methodology, 121; MacIntyre and, 56; teaching of (as response to social problems), 56

verbal ability and structure, 91-93

verbal functions, 8

verbal splendor: wild, 21

Vernon, P.: and Spearman's "g," 72; and the Das model, 93; V:Ed factor, 71-72

Vietnam, 56

violence and mass media, 83

Virtus dormitiva, 11

Von Neumann, 12

Vygotsky-Luria thesis, 109

war, 33; on poverty (U.S.A.), 63; World War Two, 10-11, 30

warehousing people, 84

Warsaw (Poland), 66

Watson, J. B., 68, 98

wealth (distribution of), 99

Weber, Max, 102

web of social reciprocity (Bruner), 33-34

Western self-consciousness, 28-29; and adaptability of Soviets, 29; Bruner (J. S.) and, 28-29

Westinghouse: evaluation of Head Start, 65

WISC, 94

Woods Hole Conference, 25-26; and national (U.S.A.) security, 26; finance for, 25-26

words: and hierarchical structures, 29-30; and realism, 30; emotionally loaded (use of), 107-108

work, 50, 79-80, 116-17, 123; downgrading of, 116; jobs, 79-80; nature of most, 50; on human science, 123; women and, 116-17

working class: proportion of population in U.S.A., 68; little seen in studies, 112

Yamani, Sheik, 30

young (the): evocation of sex-typed responses, 114

Author Index

DATE DUE

DEC 0 6 1991			
GAYLORD			PRINTED IN U.S.A.